Dictionary of Basic English

TEACHER'S GUIDE

By
Marion L. McGuire

AGS®

American Guidance Service, Inc.
Circle Pines, Minnesota 55014-1796
1-800-328-2560

Printed in the United States of America

ISBN 0-7854-1783-4

Product Number 90151

A 0 9 8 7 6 5 4 3 2 1

Contents

Introduction

The purpose of the *Teacher's Guide* for the AGS *Dictionary of Basic English* is to give students practice in using the dictionary as a reference tool for the wealth of information it contains, such as how to spell a word, where a word is divided into syllables, where a word may be hyphenated at the end of a line of writing, how to pronounce a word, where stress on a syllable should be placed in saying a word, the part or parts of speech a word may be, the various meanings of a word, examples of how words are used in phrases or sentences, and how an object may be illustrated.

Using the dictionary can serve many of these purposes. The goal is to have students reach for the dictionary when it can be useful. For that reason, most of the exercises in this program require the student to go into the dictionary to find answers. Through frequent practice, students will eventually grow in awareness of the many purposes the dictionary serves.

Do not have students memorize the information in the practice exercises. Some things will be learned by memory, but that is not the goal. Knowing what information is in the dictionary and how to find it when needed are goals of more lasting value.

—*M.L.M.*

Unit 1: The Alphabet

Unit Overview

This unit is for students who lack speed in determining what letter precedes or follows another letter. When looking for a certain letter in a dictionary, it is more efficient to know whether to go backward or forward to find the letter. Two learning aids are introduced to improve memory.

Unit Objective

• to know the order of the letters in the alphabet

Activities 1-3

Introducing the Unit

Tell students they are going to play a letter game. One student will call out a letter (for example, *G*). The first one to say the next letter of the alphabet correctly *(H)* will call out another letter (for example, *R*). When several letters have been called, the game may be changed to require saying the letter *before* the one called out.

If response is slow, introduce the Alphatape. Cut and assemble it as directed and tape it to the chalkboard. Point to any letter at random and have students say the letter before or after it, as requested. Look for improvement in speed as students become more familiar with the task.

If more help is needed, pass out copies of Activity 2, "The Alphabet Song." Explain to students that singing the letters should improve memory.

Then, discuss why it is important to know the alphabet well to use a dictionary. Have students open their dictionaries and take note of the alphabetical arrangement. Tell them to find certain letters. Make note of those who take a long time to find the right section, especially those who seem not to know whether to go forward or backward to find the letter.

Lesson 1: Alphabetical Order: Letters

Objective

• to know the order of the letters in the alphabet

Procedure

1) Write the following letters with blanks between them: l __ n, p __ r, w __ y. Ask for volunteers to fill in the blanks. Have students at their seats write the answers on scrap paper. Check responses.

2) Write the following letters with blanks on the chalkboard: __ c __, __ h __, __ t __. Ask for volunteers to fill in the blanks while students at their seats jot down the answers. Check responses.

3) Write the following alphabet frame with blanks on the chalkboard:

   a__ __ __ e__ __ __ i __ __ __ __ __ o__ __
   __ __ __ u __ __ __ __ __ __

   Ask for a volunteer to fill in the blanks between *a* and *e*. Continue in like manner until the alphabet is complete.

4) Ask if there are any questions. Determine if anyone needs more help before practice is assigned. Avoid allowing students to fail. Failure sets up a poor learning pattern that leads to lack of effort.

5) Provide small-group assistance for those who need it. Assign Activity 3, "Learning to Alphabetize," to the remainder of the class.

Unit 1 Mastery Test

The Unit 1 Mastery Test is found following the activity worksheet pages.

Unit 2: Locating Words in the Dictionary

Unit Overview

This unit begins with the Unit 1 skill of alphabetizing letters and puts it to use in locating words in a dictionary. Finding the appropriate section of the dictionary and using the guide words to locate the page both depend on skill in alphabetizing.

Unit Objectives

- to understand how words are alphabetized to the fourth letter
- to determine which words in a list fall between two guide words

Activities 4-13

Introducing the Unit

Collect several old telephone directories. Pass them out to students in various parts of the room. Have each student find his or her last name. Tear out that page for the student and pass the directory on to someone else until everyone has a page containing his or her last name. (If a name cannot be found in any directory, locate the place where the name would be alphabetically and write over that name with the student's name, using a felt-tipped pen. Do this in advance.)

Have students find the name that is alphabetically just before theirs, and the one that is just after theirs. Then have volunteers go to the chalkboard and write the three last names neatly in a column.

Example:	
1. The name before:	Duhamel
2. The student's name:	Dukes
3. The name after:	Dulac

Have students count the letters that are alike at the beginning of all three names, noting which letter is the first different letter. In this example, the third letter is the first different letter. This is the letter by which the names were alphabetized in setting up the directory. Point out how important it is to know which letter to look at (the first different letter) in seeking a word or name in an alphabetical arrangement.

Lesson 1: Alphabetical Order

Objective

- to understand how words are alphabetized to the fourth letter

Procedure

1) Write these sets of four words on the chalkboard:

Set a	Set b
runner _____	coal _____
type _____	circle _____
grief _____	clean _____
chicken _____	chunk _____

Set c	Set d
block _____	gentle _____
bran _____	geography _____
bread _____	geyser _____
blame _____	gear _____

Set e

trip _____

tribe _____

triangle _____

trick _____

Set a:

Have students look at the first letter in each word. Are these letters alike or different? **(different)** Then, put the first letters in alphabetical order. *(c, g, r, t)* All students should be working on scrap paper. Have a volunteer write the words on the chalkboard in alphabetical order on the blanks beside the words.

Set b:

Ask if the first letters in this list are alike or different. **(alike)** Have someone go to the board and underline the second letter in each word. Are these second letters alike or different? **(Different. They can be alphabetized by the second letter.)** When students finish, have a volunteer put the list on the chalkboard. Ask if there are any questions. Students should realize that words are alphabetized by the first different letter.

Set c:

This list is intended to add to that understanding. Ask students to think how this list might be alphabetized. There are two *bl* words and two *br* words. This is best handled by writing the beginning two letters in the blanks first. *(bl, bl, br, br)* Now alphabetize the *bl* words by the third letter and then do the same with the *br* words. Ask a volunteer to work at the chalkboard. Then have several students explain how to handle a mixed list such as this.

Sets d and e:

Have students discover that these lists can be alphabetized by the first different letter **(the third and fourth, respectively).** Write additional sets of words on the board if students need more help in working with letters so deep into the word. For example: *dose, dock, door, dome.* Or, *crave, crawl, crate, cramp.*

2) Summarize the lesson: Lists of words are alphabetized by the first different letter in the list. Have students explain this in their own words.

3) Ask if there are any questions. Determine if anyone needs more help before practice is assigned.

4) Provide small-group assistance for those who need it. Assign Activity 4, "Alphabetical Order: Letters" Activity 5, "The Most Familiar Meaning," Activity 6, "Alphabetical Order: Words," Activity 7, "Alphabetizing Words," and Activity 8, "Words With the Same First Letter," to the rest of the class. As practice on progressively more difficult material, assign Activity 9, "Alphabetical Order by Second Letter," Activity 10, "Alphabetical Order by Third Letter," and Activity 11, "Using the Fourth Letter to Alphabetize."

Lesson 2: Using Guide Words

Objective

- to determine which words in a list fall between two guide words

Procedure

1) Explain the term *guide words.* **(Words at the top of a dictionary page that are the same as the first and last word on a page.)** Have students open their dictionaries and find the guide words at the top of each page. Then they are to close their books.

Copy this exercise on the chalkboard:

lion	_____	lodge	_____
local	_____	liver	_____
listen	_____	location	_____
lizard	_____	linger	_____

Guide Words: **list** and **locate**

Discuss how they might know which of the eight words can be found on the pages having the guide words *list* and *locate.* Ask students to put a check mark beside a word that can be found on those pages. When students think all of the appropriate words have been checked, ask them to open their dictionaries to the page with these guide words and find the words that are on those two pages. Were the correct words checked? **(The correct words are *local, listen, lizard,* and *liver.*)**

2) Discuss whether each of the words not checked would come *before* or *after* the pages with the guide words. How does knowing alphabetical order help in this task? **(Before: *lion, linger.* After: *lodge, location.*)**

3) Ask if there are any questions. Determine if anyone needs more help before practice is assigned.

4) Provide small-group assistance for those who need it. Assign Activity 12, "Learning About Guide Words," and Activity 13, "Use the Guide Words," to the remainder of the class. Check this work on guide words as a group.

Unit 2 Mastery Test

The Unit 2 Mastery Test is found following the activity worksheet pages.

Unit 3: The Entry Word

Unit Overview

This unit begins a sequential study of parts of the dictionary entry. The entry word itself provides three pieces of information.

1) the spelling of the word

2) the division of the word into syllables by raised dots

3) with stated exceptions, the hyphenation of words at the raised dots

Unit Objectives

• to use the entry word to determine correct spelling and syllable division

• to determine where a word can be hyphenated at the end of a line

Activities 14-17

Introducing the Unit

Ask students to write these words on scrap paper:

1) *launch* (to *launch* a rocket) (page 118)

2) *cartoon* (a *cartoon* in the newspaper) (page 32)

3) *scissors* (to cut with *scissors*) (page 203)

Ask students to use the dictionary to check their spelling. Give the page numbers to anyone who can't find the word. The object is to demonstrate that words we find difficult to spell are usually not hard to find in the dictionary. It is not necessary to spoil the appearance of our work with poor spelling. Make positive comments to those who find the words and check or correct their spelling.

Tell students that they are about to learn about other ways we can use the dictionary entry word.

Lesson 1: Syllable Division and Spelling

Objective

• to use the entry word to determine correct spelling and syllable division

Procedure

1) Write the following on the chalkboard:

science   _____ _____

legislation   _____ _____

knowledge   _____ _____

bureau   _____ _____

Have students find these entry words and note how they are divided into syllables. Use the term

raised dot in describing the mark that separates the syllables. Then have volunteers write the words separated by raised dots on the long line beside each word. On the short line, write the number of syllables in the word. **(sci • ence, 2; leg • is • la • tion, 4; knowl • edge, 2; bu • reau, 2)**

2) Discuss the value of knowing where words are divided into syllables:

a. Saying a word syllable by syllable aids pronunciation.

b. Pronouncing and spelling a word syllable by syllable aid spelling.

c. It shows, with few exceptions, where a word can be hyphenated at the end of a line and carried over to the next line.

3) Ask if there are questions. Determine if anyone needs more help before practice is assigned.

4) Provide small-group assistance for those who need it. To the rest of the class, assign Activity 14, "Dividing Words Into Syllables," and Activity 15, "Counting Syllables." Check answers as a group.

Lesson 2: Syllable Division and Hyphenation

Objective

• to determine where a word can be hyphenated at the end of a line

Procedure

1) Write these words on the chalkboard:

fla • vor   set • tler   pan • try

Ask students where these words may be hyphenated if the whole word will not fit at the end of a line. **(at the raised dot)** Explain to students that, generally speaking, a word may be hyphenated at a raised dot. However, that rule has two exceptions:

a. One-letter syllables at the beginning or end of a word should not be separated from the rest of the word.

b. One-letter or two-letter endings or suffixes on words are usually not separated from the rest of the word.

2) Write these words on the chalkboard:

a • lien   read • y   tak• en
ech • o   bas • es

Ask students what to do if they come near the end of a line of writing and one of the five words above is the next word to be written. **(Accept answers.)** Could any of these words be hyphenated and carried over to the next line? **(No. The first three words have one-letter** syllables at the beginning or end of the words. The last two have two-letter endings.) What would be the correct thing to do to one of these words? **(If the whole word will not fit at the end of the line, start a new line.)**

3) Tell whether these words may be hyphenated, and if not, why not.

   e • vil **(No. One-letter syllable)**

   pan • ic **(Yes.)**

   fast • er **(No. Two-letter ending)**

4) Pass out copies of Activity 16, "Syllable Division and Hyphenation." Have a volunteer read the introductory material. Relate it to the work just done on the chalkboard.

5) Ask if there are questions. Determine if anyone needs more help before practice is assigned.

6) Provide small-group assistance for those who need it. Assign Activity 17, "Using Hyphens," to the rest of the class. Check answers as a group.

Unit 3 Mastery Test

The Unit 3 Mastery Test is found following the activity worksheet pages.

Unit 4: Using the Guide to Pronunciation

Unit Overview

This unit explains the phonetic spelling given in slashes after an entry word. The letter symbols are explained, as well as the key words in the *Guide to Pronunciation,* which are examples of how the letter symbols are pronounced. The phonetic spelling is necessary because English is not entirely phonetic. This unit is essential as an aid to pronunciation.

Unit Objectives

- to understand the form and purpose of the phonetic spelling
- to use key words to determine the sound associated with phonetic symbols
- to recognize that different letters can be associated with the same sound
- to recognize that different sounds can be associated with the same letter
- to understand the methods used to show which syllables are spoken with more stress

Activities 18-30

Introducing the Unit

The coined word *ghoti* is an example of how non-phonetic a word can be. Students may enjoy figuring out the pronunciation according to these directions. In the *Guide to Pronunciation,* find the letter symbol for each sound.

1) Pronounce the *gh* as in rou*gh*. The letter symbol for that sound is ____. *(f)*

2) Pronounce the *o* as in w*o*men. The letter symbol for that sound is ____. *(i)*

3) Pronounce the *ti* as in na*ti*on. The letter symbol for that sound is ____. *(sh)*

Ask volunteers to write in the blanks the letter symbols associated with the sounds. Ask what this coined word spells *(fish).* It would be a chore to find a real word with such an unexpected pronunciation, but thousands of words have one or more letters that stand for a different sound. The phonetic spelling helps us to pronounce these words correctly.

Lesson 1: The Phonetic Spelling

Objective

- to understand the form and purpose of the phonetic spelling

Procedure

1) Have students open their dictionaries to the first page of *A* words. Ask them to look for the phonetic spellings of the words on that page. Point out that each one is somewhat different from the entry word.

2) Introduce the *schwa*. Almost every word on page 1 has at least one schwa. Demonstrate how to make a schwa as if it were written on the face of a clock. Begin at eleven o'clock and move clockwise around the face of the clock to eight o'clock. Then draw a straight line across from eight o'clock to four o'clock. Have students trace a schwa in the air with their forefinger, then write one on paper. Students will be asked to write a few phonetic spellings later in the unit, so mastering how to write this symbol now will be helpful.

3) Ask volunteers to read a word on page 1 and decide which vowel is replaced by a schwa in the phonetic spelling. For example, in *abdomen,* schwas replace the *o* and the *e*. In *ability,* schwas replace the *a* and the second *i*. You may wish to skip the word *able,* as the final *e* is silent or unsounded. The schwa is added between the *b* and the *l* to give the letters a syllabic quality, an explanation that is beyond this program.

4) Have students turn to the *Guide to Pronunciation* on page ix. Introduce them to the terms *phonetic symbol, key word,* and *boldface type.* There are two columns of *phonetic symbols,* each followed by two or more *key words* with selected letters printed in *boldface type.* These letters have the sound of the phonetic symbol.

5) Read the key words for the schwa, noticing that all of the boldface vowels are pronounced "uh," the schwa sound. Any vowel can be pronounced as a schwa in certain syllables.

6) Pass out Activity 18, "Phonetic Spellings." Ask a volunteer to read the directions for Parts A and B. Discuss the information, relating it to the dictionary work just accomplished.

7) Ask if there are questions. Determine if anyone needs more help before proceeding.

8) Provide small-group assistance for those who need it. Assign the rest of the page to the remainder of the class. Check answers as a group.

9) Related practice: Activity 19, "The Phonetic Spelling."

Lesson 2:
Key Words and Phonetic Symbols

Objectives

• to use key words to determine the sound associated with phonetic symbols

• to recognize that different letters can be associated with the same sound

Procedure

1) Have students open their dictionaries to the *Guide to Pronunciation* on page ix. Have them find the phonetic symbol \b\, followed by the key words: **b**at, ca**bb**age, and **j**ob. Point out that all the bold-face letters look just like the phonetic symbol at the beginning of the line. That means that the sound of "b" is always made by the letter *b*.

2) Assign Activity 20, "Key Words for Phonetic Symbols." When finished, discuss what is the relationship between key words and the phonetic symbols used in this exercise. Check answers as a group.

3) Have students find the phonetic symbol "f." Notice that the "f" sound can be spelled *f, gh,* or *ph*. The letter can also be doubled. That means that the sound of "f" can be spelled in these ways. We hear an "f" sound in *laugh* and *photo* even though there is no *f* in these words. Relate this to difficulties in spelling these words.

4) Have students look up the word *laugh*. What letter symbol is used in the phonetic spelling in place of the *gh?(f)* Do the same with *photo*.

5) Have students summarize what they have learned about key words and phonetic symbols. (**Key words show the ways the sound of the phonetic symbol can be spelled. Some sounds are always spelled the same as the phonetic symbol. Other sounds have variable spellings. But, a sound is always represented by the same phonetic symbol in the phonetic spelling.**)

6) Pass out copies of Activity 21, "Symbols and Sounds." Have a volunteer read the directions of Part A. Discuss what is to be done in Part B.

7) Ask if there are questions. Determine if anyone needs more help.

8) Provide small-group assistance for those who need it. Have students do the activity.

9) Related practice: Activity 22, "Write the Phonetic Spelling."

Lesson 3:
Phonetic Symbols for Vowel Sounds

Objective

- to recognize that different sounds can be associated with the same sound letter

Procedure

1) Write the following vowel phonetic symbols on the chalkboard:

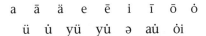

   Have students notice that although each vowel may be used two or three times, no two phonetic symbols are just alike. *Diacritical marks* (a long mark, one dot, or two dots) are used to make the vowel symbols different. Each symbol above stands for one vowel sound.

2) Have students find each vowel symbol in the *Guide to Pronunciation* and read the key words for the sound. Have students say each sound aloud as they do this.

3) Pass out copies of Activity 23, "Symbols for *A, E, I,* and *O*," which deals with symbols for vowel sounds. Ask a volunteer to read this page, stopping at each set of blanks for another volunteer to explain what should be written in that set of blanks. Continue in this manner to the bottom of the page, with students following along, but not writing.

4) Have students summarize what they have learned from this page.

   a. Vowels have more than one sound.

   b. Diacritical marks are used to indicate the different vowel sounds.

   c. The phonetic spellings have diacritical marks over the vowels, as indicated in the *Guide to Pronunciation,* so the reader can tell which sound to give the vowel.

5) Ask if there are questions. Determine if anyone needs more help.

6) Provide small-group assistance for those who need it. Assign Activity 23 to the remainder of the class. Check answers as a group.

7) Related practice: Activity 24, "Symbols for *U* and *E*," and Activity 25, "Matching Vowel Sounds."

Lesson 4:
Phonetic Symbols for Consonant Sounds

Objective

- to recognize that different sounds can be associated with the same letter

Procedure

1) Write the following words on the chalkboard: *gum, gym, jam.* Have a volunteer read the words.

   Ask: "Which two words begin with the same letter?" *(gum and gym)* "Which two words begin with the same sound?" *(gym and jam)*

2) Discuss the two sounds of *g*: a *hard* sound as in *gum* and a *soft* sound as in *gym*. **(The soft sound of *g* is the same as the "j" sound.)** Have students open their dictionaries to the word *gym* on page 95 and find its phonetic spelling. Notice that the letter symbol for *soft g* is \j\ because it sounds like *j*.

3) Have students find the \j\ letter symbol in the *Guide to Pronunciation*. Notice that *g* and *dge* also make the "j" sound.

4) Write these words on the chalkboard: *keel-coal; sell-cell.* Have a volunteer read each pair of words. Ask: "What sound does *c* have in *coal?*" **(A hard sound, the sound of "k.")** "What sound does *c* have in *cell?*" **(A soft sound, the sound of "s.")**

5) Discuss the two sounds of *c*. Then have students find the words *coal* and *cell* in their dictionaries. Ask: "What letter symbols are used for the *c's* in the phonetic spellings?" (\k\ in *coal*, \s\ in *cell*)

6) Have students look for a letter symbol for *c* in the *Guide to Pronunciation*. **(There is none.)** Discuss the reason for not having a "c" letter symbol. **(The letter *c* has no sound of its own. It makes the "k" or "s" sound.)**

7) Pass out Activity 26, "Symbols for Hard and Soft G," and Activity 27, "Symbols for Hard and Soft C. Have a volunteer read the two pages aloud, stopping at the blanks while another volunteer tells what should be written in the blanks. All students should be following along without writing.

8) Have students summarize what they have learned about the letters *c* and *g*.

9) Ask if there are any questions. Determine if anyone needs more help.

10) Provide small-group assistance for those who need it. Assign Activities 26 and 27 to the rest of the class. Check answers as a group.

11) Related practice: Activity 28, "Consonant Digraphs."

Lesson 5: Accented Syllables

Objective

• to understand the methods used to show which syllables are spoken with more stress

Procedure

1) Ask students to read the section on "Pronunciation" on page vi in their dictionaries. Discuss the use of accent marks. Have volunteers pronounce the words used in the examples: *habit, nowadays,* and *part-time.* Have them notice the difference between a bold syllable with a heavy accent mark and nonbold syllable with a light accent mark. Show this difference in the stress put on syllables.

2) Pass out Activity 29, "Syllables With Accent Marks." Have a student read the directions for Part A. Allow time for students to answer the four questions. **(The answers can be found at the top of the page.)** Check answers as a group.

3) Have a volunteer read the directions for Part B. Allow time for students to look up the phonetic spelling of *aspect* and mark the accented syllable. Discuss the question. **(The heavier accent is on the first syllable.)**

4) Ask if there are any questions.

5) Have students do the fifth question on the worksheet. Copy this chart on the chalkboard:

Entry Word	Phonetic Spelling	Accented Syllable
dinner	_____\\	_____
pattern	_____\\	_____
sandwich	_____\\	_____
giraffe	_____\\	_____
recover	_____\\	_____

Have students copy this format on the back of Activity 29 or on a blank sheet of paper. Then have them copy the phonetic spelling in the second column. In the last column, they should tell whether the first or second syllable is accented. (first, first, first, second, second) Check answers as a group.

6) Related practice: Activity 30, "Accented Syllables."

Unit Mastery Test

The Unit 4 Mastery Test is found following the activity worksheet pages.

Unit 5: Parts of Speech

Unit Overview

This unit acquaints students with the idea that a word can function as more than one part of speech, each having slightly different meanings. To choose the correct meaning of a word in a sentence, identifying its part of speech is most helpful.

Unit Objectives

• to know the function of each part of speech
• to identify the part of speech of a word in a sentence

Activities 31-33

Introducing the Unit

Ask students to find the word *exact* on page 73 of their dictionaries. Have someone read the two definitions of the word, one as a verb (**to demand**) and the other as an adjective (**accurate**). Notice how different these meanings are—so different that one should not be confused with the other. Write and study these sentences on the board:

1) Herb drew an *exact* copy of the artist's work.
2) Landlords *exact* the payment of rent from their tenants.

Ask: "What is the meaning of *exact* in each sentence? (1: accurate; 2: to demand) Why is it easier to find the correct meaning if you know that *exact* is a verb in one sentence and an adjective in the other? **(It saves time in finding a meaning that makes sense.)** Would it make sense to say: 'Landlords *accurate* the payment'? **(No.)** 'Herb drew a *demand* copy'? **(No.)** Try the definitions the other way around." The meaning chosen must always make sense.

Lesson 1:
The Abbreviations and Functions of Parts of Speech

Objective

• to know the function of each part of speech

Procedure

1) Have students open their dictionaries to page vi and find the heading "Word Meanings." Ask students to read to the end of that section. Then, discuss the eight parts of speech and functions as given on page vi.

2) Pass out copies of Activity 31, "Functions of the Parts of Speech." Have a volunteer read the directions. Then have students fill in the blanks. Check as a group.

Lesson 2:
Choosing the Correct Part of Speech

Objective

- to identify the part of speech of a word in a sentence

Procedure

1) Pass out copies of Activity 32, "Many Parts of Speech." Have a volunteer read the directions. Discuss what is to be done on the page.

2) Have students find the word *lock* in their dictionaries on page 124. Then, have them locate the parts of speech for which meanings are given (**noun and verb**) The answer is written on the exercise as an example.

3) Have students look up the next word, *since,* and write the parts of speech on the line provided. (**adverb, preposition, and conjunction**)

4) Ask if there are any questions. Determine if anyone needs more help.

5) Provide small-group assistance for those who need it while the remainder of the class finishes the page. Check answers as a group.

6) Pass out copies of Activity 33, "Choosing the Correct Part of Speech." Have someone read the directions. Work through numbers 1 and 2 together. *For students who cannot understand parts of speech, have them substitute each meaning in the sentence to see which one makes sense, and then write the part of speech of that meaning.*

7) Ask students to complete the page, answering questions as needed. Check answers as a group.

Unit 5 Mastery Test

The Unit 5 Mastery Test is found following the activity worksheet pages.

Unit 6: Inflected Forms of Words

Unit Overview

There are standard rules for adding endings to nouns, adjectives, adverbs, and verbs. These rules apply to most inflected forms.

This unit reviews these rules and applies them to writing regular and irregular inflected forms.

Unit Objectives

- to know the form and purpose of inflectional endings
- to recognize the spelling rules that cause some inflected forms of words to be irregular
- to apply the spelling rules in writing inflected forms of words

Activities 34-42

Introducing the Unit

Write the following exercise on the chalkboard.

- **a.** one French fry, a dish of French ____ (**fries**)
- **b.** one die, two____ (**dice**)
- **c.** one mouse, two ____ (**mice**)
- **d.** one mosquito, two ____ (**mosquitoes**)
- **e.** one shelf, two ____ (**shelves**)
- **f.** That is lengthy, but this is ____. (**lengthier**)
- **g.** Every day I chop wood.
  Yesterday I ____ wood. (**chopped**)

Ask student volunteers to read across a line, saying and spelling the form of the word that belongs in the blank. Then have them think where they might have found the words that belong in the blanks, especially if they had trouble spelling them.

In this unit students will learn three simple rules to spell many words with endings. Also, they will find that many of these words with endings are given in the dictionary entry.

Lesson 1:
Inflectional Endings and Their Purpose

Objective

- to know the form and purpose of inflectional endings

Procedure

1) Pass out copies of Activity 34, "Words With Endings." Ask a volunteer to read the directions. Have students open their dictionaries to page vii and find the place described in the directions.

Review what they will be looking for as they read. **(The parts of speech that have endings, the endings that are added to each part of speech, and the purpose of the ending.)**

2) Ask students to scan pages vii and viii, and look for boldface headings that name parts of speech. Students may skip *pronouns* at this time. They will be dealt with in Unit 9. They will find *nouns, adjectives, adverbs,* and *verbs* discussed in this section. Ask students to write these four parts of speech in the left column on their activity sheet.

3) Have students go back to each section for information about the endings.

4) Ask if there are questions and determine if anyone needs help before the group works on the assignment.

5) Provide small-group assistance for those who need it, while the rest of the class finishes the assignment. Check work as a group.

6) Related Practice: Activity 35, "Regular Inflected Forms."

Lesson 2:
Irregular Inflected Forms of Words

Objective

- to recognize the spelling rules that cause some inflected forms of words to be irregular

Procedure

1) Pass out copies of Activity 36, "Irregular Inflected Forms of Words." Ask a volunteer to read the directions. Have students open their dictionaries to page vii. The last paragraph explains three types of words that change in spelling when an ending is added. Discuss the text of the last paragraph and relate it to the words *big, noble,* and *tasty.* Then ask students to state three rules by completing these sentences. Write them on the chalkboard.

   1. When a word ends in a single consonant preceded by a single vowel, . . .
   2. When a word ends in silent *-e,* . . .
   3. When a word ends in *-y* preceded by a consonant, . . .

2) Write the following words on the chalkboard for practice in applying the rules. Ask students to spell the forms requested and to tell which rule applies: **the plural of** berry, **the comparative and superlative of** flat , **the past tense and past participle of** cable.

   Use these sentences as examples if students have difficulty remembering the forms:

   I bought a box of *berries.* **(Rule 3)**

This is the *flattest* stone of all. **(Rule 1)**

John *cabled* his uncle yesterday. **(Rule 2)**

He is *cabling* all his relatives. **(Rule 2)**

3) Use the following words for additional practice: poppy **(the plural)**, idle **(the comparative and superlative forms)**, occupy **(the past tense and past participle)**.

   Note: Students who have difficulty may look up the words in their dictionaries.

4) Pass out copies of Activity 37, "Irregular Adjectives and Adverbs." Ask a volunteer to read the directions. Discuss what is to be done on the page.

5) Ask if there are questions and determine if anyone needs more help.

6) Provide small-group assistance for those who need it while the remainder of the class completes the assignment.

7) Activity 38, "Final *Y* Spelling Rule," and Activity 39, "Irregular Inflected Nouns," may be used as additional assignments on subsequent days.

Lesson 3:
Irregular Inflected Forms of Verbs

Objective

- to apply the spelling rules in writing inflected forms of words

Procedure

1) Pass out copies of Activity 40, "Regular and Irregular Verbs." Ask a volunteer to read the directions. Discuss what is to be done. Complete the first question. Then have students find the word *work* on page 273 in their dictionaries. Ask them to look for the word *verb* in the entry, followed by the irregular forms. Students should be aware that irregular forms of words are given in boldface type immediately after the part of speech.

2) Ask if there are any questions and then allow time for the class to complete the blanks on the page. Check as a group, asking students to explain the spelling rule applied to each verb.

3) Activity 41, "Final *E* Spelling Rule," and Activity 42, "Irregular Verbs," may be used on subsequent days. Students should use their dictionaries to make sure words are spelled correctly. As work is checked as a group, students should explain the spelling rule that applies.

Unit 6 Mastery Test

The Unit 6 Mastery Test is found following the activity worksheet pages.

Unit 7: Getting the Meaning of Words

Unit Overview

This unit is focused on using all that the dictionary has to offer in getting a clear meaning for an entry word. The part of speech of the word, the context in which it is found, and the illustrations and examples all assist the reader in using the dictionary to full advantage. The activities enable the student to practice full dictionary usage and to experience its benefits.

Unit Objectives

- to consider the part of speech in selecting a meaning that makes sense in the sentence where the word is found
- to be aware of words that look alike but have different meanings (homographs)
- to use illustrations to enhance the meaning of the dictionary definitions they represent
- to use the examples in the dictionary entry as a model of how the word can be used

Activities 43-47

Introducing the Unit

Write the following sentences on the chalkboard:

a. Mr. Johnson is a *pillar* of our community. Ask: "What does that sentence say about Mr. Johnson? What is a *pillar?* How does it apply to a person? Look up the word *pillar* and then explain the sentence."

b. St. Louis is the *hub* for that airline. Ask: "What does *hub* mean in this sentence? Find *hub* in your dictionary."

c. The animals are *native* to the North Temperate *Zone.* Ask: "What does *native* mean? Check the meaning in your dictionary. What does *zone* mean in this sentence?"

Help students to become aware that the dictionary is a resource they can frequently turn to. This unit will review some ways it can be used to bring meaning to our language usage.

Lesson 1: A Meaning for the Correct Part of Speech

Objective

- to consider the part of speech in selecting a meaning that makes sense in the sentence where the word is found

Procedure

1) Write these sentences on the chalkboard:

   a. My father said that March is the prime time for planting peas.

   Ask a volunteer to read the sentence. Have students look up *prime.* Determine what part of speech *prime* is. (**adjective; it modifies time.**) Now tell what *prime* means in that sentence. (**first in importance**)

   b. The hunters had to **prime** the water pump in the cabin. (**Proceed as with *prime*. It is a verb meaning: "to get the pump ready to operate."**) Help students to realize that they have the correct meaning when it makes sense in the sentence.

2) Pass out copies of Activity 43, "Finding the Part of Speech and Meaning." Ask a volunteer to read the directions. If the class is weak in parts of speech, it may be better to do the whole page as a group. In that case, it may be necessary to rely upon the meaning that makes sense in the sentence, checking the meanings of all parts of speech given. If students work independently, check work as a group.

3) Activity 44, "Choosing a Meaning," may be used on a subsequent day. With only two parts of speech to consider, the problem of choice is much less difficult. Check work as a group.

Lesson 2: Homographs

Objective

- to be aware of words that look alike but have different meanings (homographs)

Procedure

1) Write *row* twice on the chalkboard.

   Ask students to find these words in the dictionary (page 198) and copy the phonetic spelling (rō) and (raú). Choose a volunteer to pronounce the two words. Ask: "Do the two words look alike? (**Yes**) Do they sound alike? (**No**) Are they alike in meaning? (**No**) We call words that look alike but have different meanings *homographs*. Homographs may or may not be pronounced alike."

   Read these sentences:

   a. It made my arms ache to *row* so far. Ask: "What part of speech is *row?* (**verb**) What does it mean?" (**to move a boat through the water by using oars**)

   b. There was a **row** in the parking lot until the police arrived. Ask: "How is *row* pronounced in this sentence? (**raú**) What part of speech is it? (**noun**) What does it mean?" (**a noisy fight**)

2) Ask a volunteer to explain *homographs.* (**two words that look alike but are different in meaning and sometimes in pronunciation**)

3) Pass out copies of Activity 45, "Homographs: Alike but Different." Ask a volunteer to read the directions for Part A. Then read and discuss the directions for Part B. Allow time for the work to be completed. Then, check as a group. Discuss any difficulties.

Lesson 3: The Use of Illustrations

Objective

• to use illustrations to enhance the meaning of the dictionary definitions they represent

Procedure

1) Ask students to find the following entry words in their dictionaries.

a. clipper	**c.** fan	**e.** latitude
b. coral	**d.** junk	**f.** target

For each word, read the definition and study the illustration. Then, ask a volunteer to describe what is in the illustration that is not described in words. How does the illustration add to the definition?

2) Pass out copies of Activity 46, "The Use of Illustrations." Ask a volunteer to read the directions. Then, have the class open their dictionaries to the word *pulley* (page 177) and study the illustration. Ask if anyone wants to add something to the description given beside the word on their paper.

3) Assign the remaining three words: *helicopter, lizard,* and *serpent.* Share answers as a group, allowing for differences in responses.

Lesson 4: The Use of Examples

Objective

• to use the examples in the dictionary entry as a model of how the word can be used

Procedure

1) Ask students to find the word *rough* in their dictionaries. The five definitions for *rough* as an adjective have examples that are not complete sentences:

1) *rough* road	4) *rough* character
2) *rough* voice	5) *rough* texture
3) *rough* seas	

Ask students to write one sentence on scrap paper using each of these examples. Have them circle each of the examples.

2) Give several students an opportunity to read the sentences they wrote for each example.

3) Ask students why they think examples are given in the dictionary entry. (**To make the meaning clearer**) A student may read a definition and still not know how to use the word in a phrase or sentence. The example puts the word into a common expression they might say or hear.

4) Pass out copies of Activity 47, "Examples Help." Ask a volunteer to read the directions for Parts A and B. Allow time for the work to be completed. Check answers as a group.

Unit 7 Mastery Test

The Unit 7 Mastery Test is found following the activity worksheet pages.

Unit 8: Using the Dictionary to Improve Vocabulary

Unit Overview

This unit explores a few of the ways students might add to their vocabulary. Interest in any phase of learning is more often "caught" than taught. This is especially true of vocabulary. Most students are comfortable communicating in their present vocabulary, no matter how limited, until something or someone comes along to stimulate for them a fascination with words.

Unit Objectives

* to display an interest in new words
* to consider several sources of new words
* to regularly add new words to student's vocabulary

Activities 48-50

Introducing the Unit

Try some of these activities to build students' interest in words:

1) Writing poetry is a fine vehicle for increasing interest in words. Try writing a short poem such as a haiku or diamante as a class project. It may be helpful to read some poetry to the class before starting the writing project. *Haiku* is a Japanese form of poetry that always refers to a single event in nature. It has three lines and seventeen syllables, as follows:

Example:
The wise old owl waits **(five syllables)**
Until the world goes to sleep **(seven syllables)**
And then eats his lunch. **(five syllables)**

Diamante is another poetry form that provides the occasion for a search for interesting words and expressions. It has seven lines, beginning and ending with opposites:

Example:
Rain **(noun)**
Heavy, cold **(adjective, adjective)**
Drenching, driving, biting **(participle, participle, participle)**
Puddles, umbrellas, sunglasses, reflections **(noun, noun, noun, noun)**
Shining, radiating, dazzling **(participle, participle, participle)**
Bright, warm **(adjective, adjective)**
Sun **(noun—opposite of Line 1)**

This poem divides in the middle of line 4. The first half describes the first noun *(rain)*, the second half describes the last noun *(sun)*. It invites the use of words that paint pictures in the mind, an obvious aid to vocabulary development.

When students understand haiku and diamante, they may wish to write their own poems, perhaps putting together a collection for classroom reading.

2) Music is another form of expression that provides opportunities for sharing ideas about words. Consider songs with descriptive passages. For example, have the class sing "America the Beautiful." The words are:

Oh, beautiful for spacious skies, for amber waves of grain.
For purple mountain majesties above the fruited plain.
America! America! God shed His grace on thee. And crown thy good with brotherhood,
From sea to shining sea.

This song has wonderful visual images. Invite students to share the pictures that come to mind as they sing . . . for spacious skies . . . waves of grain . . . the fruited plain . . . from sea to shining sea . . .

Ask students to sing the song again, bringing to mind the colorful pictures that the words describe. When students have the opportunity to become creative, many of them develop a real interest in the words they use to describe their thoughts.

Ask students to think of colorful descriptions of the part of America in which they live.

Invite students to bring in the words of songs that have descriptive words they would like to learn. Be sure to look over the songs before they learn or share them.

3) Read literature. Students should be read to at least ten minutes every day from a poem or story that evokes their interest and emotional involvement. Occasionally, write a beautiful or gripping word from the reading on the chalkboard and talk about it. Use the dictionary to expand its meaning for the class. Perhaps students will add it to their new vocabulary list.

4) Tell students that they will have an opportunity to add interesting new words to their vocabularies that will improve their reading, writing, and speaking. Use a notebook page. Ask students to find at least one new word a day that they would like to learn and record it with a short definition.

Lesson 1: Adding to the Meaning of Words

Objective

- to display an interest in words

Procedure

1) Review the motivational activities that have been conducted and ask students to share any new words they have found to add to their vocabulary. Make only positive comments.

2) Pass out copies of Activity 48, "Adding to the Meaning of Words." Ask a volunteer to read the directions.

   Explain to students that we often find words that have several definitions. Some are quite familiar, but others are not. Read the directions and complete the exercise.

3) Allow time for the work to be done. Invite some students to write sentences on the chalkboard using the meanings they have written.

4) Ask if students would like to add one of these words to their vocabulary lists.

5) Related practice: Activity 49, "The Least Familiar Meaning."

Lesson 2: Developing Background for Word Meaning

Objectives

- to consider several sources of new words
- regularly add new words to students' vocabulary

Procedure

1) Discuss with students the ongoing experiences in their lives that are sources of new words. Write a few topics with suggestions, such as the following:

   Talents—music, art, science . . .

   Abilities—athletics, handwork . . .

   Interests—sports events, TV shows, cooking . . .

   Ask students to add topics or suggestions following the topics that would include their talents, abilities, and interests. Then, ask students to give some words that they have learned because of their participation in such activities, words that are specific to that field. List these on the chalkboard and give students a little time to talk about their words. Be enthusiastic about student contributions. Point out that these activities are an ongoing source of new words that will help them to read, write, and talk about the things that most interest them.2) Discuss the value of reading stories and poems as a source of interesting words. For example, suppose they read the following sentences in a story. Which words would help them to build images in their minds about what was happening?

   a. Tom's scanty supplies were sheltered under a makeshift tent.

   b. There was something mysterious about the deep, narrow place in the river, overhung with the low-slung boughs of a giant pine.

   c. The wind shifted and the beetles stirred in the garden, making a whirring noise.

3) Explore student interest in *etymology,* the history of words. A well-known example is the word *sandwich,* named after the fourth Earl of Sandwich, who is supposed to have invented it. While learning a large number of words through word histories is not possible, it certainly adds interest and makes the words learned in this manner more memorable. It may be possible to find library books on etymology.

4) Encourage students to write lists of new words they are learning. Check on their lists. Encourage a sharing of information about where new words are found. Allow time for students to report in a few sentences about what literature they have found interesting to read. Find out if the library has high-interest, low-vocabulary books for those who need them. Ask students what things *you* have read aloud that they have enjoyed.

5) Related practice: Activity 50, "The Most Familiar Meaning."

Unit 8 Mastery Test

The Unit 8 Mastery Test (which is really a report, due to the personal nature of the material) is found following the activity worksheet pages.

Unit 9: Using the Appendixes

Unit Overview

Many students are unaware of the helpful information often found in the appendixes of textbooks and reference books. The activities in this unit will acquaint them with the types of information to be found in the dictionary and give them an opportunity to become accustomed to using the appendixes.

Unit Objectives

- to be aware that cardinal and ordinal numbers are listed in Appendix A
- to understand that personal, demonstrative, indefinite, relative, compound relative, and interrogative pronouns are listed in Appendix B
- to know that the conjugations of the verbs *to have* and *to be* are listed in Appendix C
- to understand that the most common irregular verbs are listed in Appendix C
- to be aware that sixty commonly misspelled English words are found in Appendix D

Activities 51-63

Introducing the Unit

1) Write the following on the chalkboard:

a. 1,602,009.4 Say: "Read this number orally. See page 282 for where the *and* should be included." (**one million, six hundred two thousand, nine and four-tenths**)

b. They wanted to do the work ____. Ask: "What pronoun should be put in the blank? See page 283 for alternatives." (**themselves**)

c. By the time Paul graduates, he ____ ____ ____ in school for fourteen years. Say: "Use a form of the verb *to be*. The answer can be found on page 285." (**will have been**)

d. I thought she could bear this pain because she has ____ worse pains in the past. (See page 286 for *borne*.)

e. The (libary, library) has many interesting books and magazines. Say: "Look at page 287 for the correct spelling." (**library**)

2) Ask a volunteer to read one of the above. If an answer is incorrect, have the class open their dictionaries to the page on which the answer can be found and guide them to the correct answer through questioning. Point out to students that they might be able to use the appendixes on many occasions.

Lesson 1: Cardinal and Ordinal Numbers

Objective

- to be aware that cardinal and ordinal numbers are listed in Appendix A

Procedure

1) Ask students to open their dictionaries to page 281. Ask one volunteer to read the numbers from one to ten, and another to read the numbers from eleven to twenty. Ask: "What is in the slashes after each number?" (**the word's pronunciation**)

2) Write several whole numbers on the chalkboard and ask volunteers to read them. Warn them against the use of *and* within a whole number. See the bottom of page 281.

3) Write several whole numbers followed by fractions or decimals (such as 23.53 or 31 3/4) and ask volunteers to read them. Notice whether they use *and* correctly. See the top of page 282.

4) Talk about ordinal numbers. They refer to things listed in *order* or sequence such as "*twelfth* in line," or the "*twentieth* day of the month." Write several ordinal numbers (10th, 3d, etc.) and have students read them. See page 282.

5) Pass out copies of Activity 51, "Reading Cardinal Numbers." Have a volunteer read the directions for Parts A and B. Allow students to use the dictionary as a resource. Check answers as a group.

6) Related practice: Activity 53, "Reading Ordinal Numbers"

Lesson 2: Pronouns

Objective

- to understand that personal, demonstrative, indefinite, relative, compound relative, and interrogative pronouns are listed in Appendix B

Procedure

1) Ask students to open their dictionaries to page 283. Then choose a volunteer to read across the row of personal pronouns indicated, as follows:

a. 1st person singular—(I, my, mine, me, myself)

Have students select from these pronouns to fill the blanks in the following sentence.

I left ____ jacket on the bench, so ____ went back to get it ____. (**my, I myself**)

b. 2d person plural—(you, your, yours, you, yourselves)

Have students select from these pronouns to fill the blanks in the following sentence.

These jackets are ____. You put them here ____. I know they belong to ____. (**yours, yourself, you**)

2) Ask students to look at the demonstrative pronouns on page 283 and read them. Then use them in the blanks in this sentence: ____ are prettier than those birds, and ____ one is the prettiest of all. **(these, this)**

3) Have students identify the indefinite pronouns in these sentences. See page 283.

   Both of the twins have several of these plastic containers, yet neither will loan us one to take on the picnic. **(both, several, neither, one)**

   Someone should teach them to cook something. **(someone, something)**

   Everyone thinks that is a good idea, but nobody does anything about it. **(everyone, nobody, anything)**

4) Fill in the blanks with an interrogative pronoun. See page 284, bottom.

   a. ____ coat is this? **(Whose)**

   b. ____ called my name? **(Who)**

   c. To ____ do you wish to speak? **(whom)**

   d. ____ time is it? **(What)**

5) Ask if there are questions about any of the pronouns. Point out that Appendix B lists the various kinds of pronouns. Students can become familiar with them and refer to them when needed.

6) Pass out copies of Activity 53, "Personal Pronouns." Have someone read the directions and then allow time for the work to be done. Activity 54, "Demonstrative and Interrogative Pronouns," and Activity 55, "Relative Pronouns," may be used as follow-up activities on subsequent days.

Lesson 3: Helping and Linking Verbs

Objective

• to know that the conjugations of the verbs *to have* and *to be* are listed in Appendix C

Procedure

1) Ask students to open their dictionaries to page 285. Review with students the conjugation of the verb *to have,* giving attention to the various tenses.

2) Point out that the conjugation of the verb *to be* is also on page 285. Review with students when each of the tenses would be used.

3) Pass out copies of Activity 56, "The Verb *to Have.*" Ask someone to read the directions. Discuss what is meant by the "question form" of the verb. Allow time for the work to be completed. Check the work as a group.

4) Pass out copies of Activity 58, "The Verb *to Be.*" Ask students to follow the same procedure as above.

5) Related practice: Activity 57, "Six Tenses of *to Have,*" and Activity 59, "Six Tenses of *to Be.*"

Lesson 4: Irregular Verbs

Objective

• to understand that the most common irregular verbs are listed in Appendix C

Procedure

1) Pass out copies of Activity 60, "Irregular Verbs." Ask a volunteer to read the directions for Parts A and B. Turn to page 286 in the dictionary and have several students read the principal parts of a verb selected at random.

2) Ask students if they have any questions about the principal parts of these verbs and how to identify them. Allow time for students to complete the page and then check Part A as a group. Invite students to share their responses for the sentences in Part B. Have students complete Part C. Check answers as a group.

3) Copies of Activity 61, "Using Irregular Verbs," may be used on a subsequent day.

Lesson 5: Commonly Misspelled English Words

Objective

• to be aware that sixty commonly misspelled English words are found in Appendix D

Procedure

1) Pass out copies of Activity 62, "Learning to Correct Misspelled Words." Have a volunteer read the directions for Part A.

2) Have students complete the activity with the help of Appendix D, page 287 in the dictionary, if needed. Allow students time to complete the sentences in Part B.

3) Hand out copies of Activity 63, "Words That Cause Trouble." Discuss the directions to be sure everyone understands what they are to do.

4) Allow students time to complete the activity. They may work together in small groups or use page 287 in the dictionary for help.

Unit 9 Mastery Test

The Unit 9 Mastery Test is found following the activity worksheet pages.

The Alphatape

Directions: Cut on the dotted lines. Tape pieces together to make an Alphatape.

a b c d e f g

h i j k l m n

o p q r s t u

v w x y z

The Alphabet Song

Directions: Try singing the alphabet to see how much easier it is to remember which letter comes next.

a   b   c   d   e   f   g   h   i   j   k   l   m   n   o   p,

q   r   s   t   u   v   w   —   —   x   y   and   z.

Now you know your   a   b   c's. You can use the   dic-tion-ar - y!

Dictionary of Basic English

Learning to Alphabetize

A. *Directions:* Write a letter in each blank to complete the alphabet.

a b c ___ ___ ___ ___ ___ i ___ ___ ___ ___ n

___ ___ ___ ___ s ___ ___ ___ w ___ ___ z

The Alphabet

a b c d e f g h i j k l m n o p q r s t u v w x y z

B. *Directions:* Fill in each blank with the letter that comes *between* the two letters given.

1) h ___ j	**9)** w ___ y	**17)** a ___ c
2) g ___ i	**10)** p ___ r	**18)** k ___ m
3) u ___ w	**11)** t ___ v	**19)** o ___ q
4) n ___ p	**12)** q ___ s	**20)** j ___ l
5) d ___ f	**13)** e ___ g	**21)** x ___ z
6) l ___ n	**14)** b ___ d	**22)** i ___ k
7) m ___ o	**15)** v ___ x	**23)** f ___ h
8) c ___ e	**16)** r ___ t	**24)** s ___ u

Dictionary of Basic English

Alphabetical Order: Letters

A. *Directions:* Fill in each blank with the letter that comes *between* the two given letters.

1) r ____ t

2) m ____ o

3) u ____ w

4) l ____ n

5) v ____ x

6) k ____ m

7) i ____ k

8) a ____ c

9) b ____ d

10) o ____ q

11) d ____ f

12) x ____ z

13) f ____ h

14) s ____ u

15) p ____ r

16) w ____ y

17) q ____ s

18) t ____ v

19) n ____ p

20) e ____ g

21) c ____ e

22) j ____ l

23) g ____ i

24) h ____ j

B. *Directions:* Fill in each blank to complete the alphabet.

a b c ____ ____ ____ ____ ____ i ____ ____ ____ ____ n

____ ____ ____ ____ s ____ ____ ____ w ____ ____ z

C. *Directions:* Write the alphabet on the lines below.

_____

_____

_____

Dictionary of Basic English

The Most Familiar Meaning

Directions: Look up each of the following words in your dictionary. Use the phonetic spelling to help you pronounce it correctly. Then, read the definitions. Choose a meaning for each word with which you are most familiar. Write a sentence using each meaning you choose. The first one has been done for you.

Words	Sentences
1) extend	_____
	_____
2) fantasy	_____
	_____
3) fierce	_____
	_____
4) fortune	_____
	_____
5) foul	_____
	_____
6) fowl	_____
	_____
7) freight	_____
	_____
8) fresh	_____
	_____

Dictionary of Basic English

Alphabetical Order: Words

Directions: In the dictionary, words are arranged alphabetically. To use the dictionary well, seeing where words belong in an alphabetical arrangement is important. Write each set of words in alphabetical order.

Set 1

parade   _____

civil   _____

route   _____

guide   _____

letter   _____

brave   _____

Set 2

near   _____

announce   _____

hammer   _____

report   _____

orbit   _____

cause   _____

Set 3

unit   _____

tender   _____

wind   _____

bench   _____

vacant   _____

purple   _____

Set 4

fin   _____

note   _____

plane   _____

mistake   _____

laundry   _____

camel   _____

Dictionary of Basic English

Alphabetizing Words

Directions: Words are alphabetically arranged in the dictionary. To use the dictionary well, seeing where words belong in an alphabetical arrangement is important. Write these words in alphabetical order.

trunk _____

zipper _____

serve _____

low _____

nickel _____

elbow _____

idea _____

basic _____

alley _____

mail _____

rip _____

fare _____

week _____

diary _____

clay _____

Dictionary of Basic English

Words With the Same First Letter

Directions: To put these words in alphabetical order, look at the second letter. Write each set of words in alphabetical order.

Set 1

by   _____

bluff   _____

button   _____

bowl   _____

birthday   _____

beetle   _____

bring   _____

Set 2

dinner   _____

dome   _____

dance   _____

drum   _____

dear   _____

Dictionary of Basic English

Alphabetical Order by Second Letter

Directions: When words begin with the same letter, they are put into alphabetical order by the second letter. Look at the second letter of each word to put each each set of words in alphabetical order. Write the words on the lines.

Set 1

cough _____

class _____

cent _____

curve _____

cavity _____

civil _____

Set 2

govern _____

gauge _____

ginger _____

guide _____

gentle _____

gym _____

Set 3

bake _____

brave _____

bundle _____

blanket _____

bend _____

book _____

Set 4

mustard _____

mention _____

magic _____

mole _____

myth _____

mind _____

Dictionary of Basic English

Alphabetical Order by Third Letter

Directions: Words that begin with the same two letters must be put into alphabetical order by the third letter. Write each set of words in alphabetical order.

Set 1

loud _____

lofty _____

lobster _____

lodge _____

love _____

long _____

Set 2

together _____

toll _____

torch _____

tomato _____

toe _____

topic _____

today _____

Dictionary of Basic English

Using the Fourth Letter to Alphabetize

Directions: When words begin with the same three letters, they are put into alphabetical order by the fourth letter. Write each set of words in alphabetical order.

Set 1

sport   _____

spoil   _____

spout   _____

spool   _____

spoke   _____

spot   _____

Set 2

these   _____

then   _____

they   _____

theater   _____

their   _____

there   _____

Learning About Guide Words

Directions: Guide words are given for each set of words below. On the line before each word, write *Yes* if the word can be found on the pages having those guide words. Write *No* if the word cannot be found on the pages having those guide words.

Set 1

Guide words: *list* and *locate*

1) _____ lion

2) _____ listen

3) _____ locomotive

4) _____ local

5) _____ lizard

6) _____ linger

7) _____ lodge

8) _____ location

9) _____ liver

10) _____ loaf

Set 2

Guide words: *minority* and *moccasin*

1) _____ mingle

2) _____ missile

3) _____ moment

4) _____ mixture

5) _____ mirror

6) _____ million

7) _____ moose

8) _____ monarch

9) _____ moan

10) _____ mist

Dictionary of Basic English

Use the Guide Words

Directions: Two guide words are given in **boldface type** at the top of each page of the dictionary. The guide words are the same as the first and last word on the page. Using the guide words lets us know whether a word falls alphabetically between the two guide words.

Guide words are given for each set of words below. On the line before each word, write *Yes* if the word can be found on the pages having those guide words. Write *No* if the word cannot be found on the pages having those guide words.

Set 1

Guide words: *sea* and *section*

1) _____ segment

2) _____ seafarer

3) _____ secret

4) _____ scrub

5) _____ second

6) _____ search

7) _____ scheme

8) _____ senior

9) _____ seaweed

10) _____ session

Set 2

Guide words: *theory* and *this*

1) _____ through

2) _____ thief

3) _____ thrill

4) _____ thumb

5) _____ thirst

6) _____ thread

7) _____ thing

8) _____ thigh

9) _____ thought

10) _____ there

Dictionary of Basic English

Dividing Words Into Syllables

Directions: Each entry word in the dictionary, given in **boldface type**, is spelled correctly and divided into syllables by raised dots.

Look up these entry words in the dictionary. Write each word as it is written in your dictionary with raised dots dividing the syllables. Be sure to spell the words correctly. Write the number of syllables in each word. The first one has been done for you.

		Entry Word	**Number of Syllables**
1)	flannel	*flan • nel*	*2*
2)	grasshopper	_____	_____
3)	fiction	_____	_____
4)	chocolate	_____	_____
5)	maintenance	_____	_____
6)	radiation	_____	_____
7)	survival	_____	_____
8)	handwriting	_____	_____
9)	building	_____	_____
10)	triumph	_____	_____

Dictionary of Basic English

Counting Syllables

Directions: Look up these entry words in the dictionary. Write each word as it is written in your dictionary with raised dots dividing the syllables. Be sure to spell the words correctly. Write the number of syllables in each word. The first one has been done for you.

		Entry Word	**Number of Syllables**
1)	ability	*a • bil • i • ty*	*4*
2)	dinosaur		
3)	dome		
4)	kerosene		
5)	obedience		
6)	paddle		
7)	population		
8)	porpoise		
9)	ultraviolet		
10)	windmill		

Syllable Division and Hyphenation

Directions: The raised dots in the entry word show where the word is divided into syllables. Since words can be hyphenated only between syllables, the raised dots also show where a word can be divided with a hyphen at the end of a line and finished on the next line. There are two exceptions to this rule.

1. One-letter syllables at the beginning or end of a word should not be separated from the rest of the word.
2. One- or two-letter endings are usually not separated from the word.

Write *Yes* on the line beside each word if it may be divided and hyphenated at the raised dot. Write *No* if the word may not be hyphenated at the raised dot. If your answer is *No*, tell why not. The first two have been done for you.

	Yes or No?	**If No, Why Not?**
1) pop • corn	*Yes*	
2) var • y	*No*	*Don't separate a one-letter syllable from the rest of the word*
3) ci • ty	_____	_____
4) a • mong	_____	_____
5) dis • gust	_____	_____
6) eas • y	_____	_____
7) beau • ty	_____	_____
8) dai • ry	_____	_____

Using Hyphens

Directions: Write *Yes* on the line beside each word if it may be divided and hyphenated at the raised dot at the end of a line of writing. Write *No* if the word may not be hyphenated at the raised dot. If your answer is *No*, tell why not.

	Yes or No?	**If No, Why Not?**
1) gen • tly	_____	_____
2) u • nion	_____	_____
3) week • end	_____	_____
4) o • cean	_____	_____
5) nois • y	_____	_____
6) cous • in	_____	_____
7) del • ta	_____	_____
8) crook • ed	_____	_____

Dictionary of Basic English

Phonetic Spellings

A. Directions: Phonetic spellings are given as an aid to pronunciation. They are found in slashes after each entry word in the dictionary.

The phonetic spelling is written in symbols. The phonetic symbols are listed in the *Guide to Pronunciation* on page ix of your dictionary. Many of the symbols are also shown on the bottom right of each set of two pages. The phonetic symbols are followed by key words. The key words have letters in **boldface type** that have the sound of the phonetic symbol. Answer the following questions.

1) Why are phonetic spellings given in the dictionary? _____

_____

2) Where are the phonetic spellings found? _____

_____

3) How is the phonetic spelling written? _____

_____

4) Where can you look to find out how to pronounce the phonetic symbols? _____

_____

5) How do the key words help in pronouncing the phonetic symbols? _____

_____

B. Directions: Look up the phonetic spelling of *aisle*. Write it in the slashes after the word. Then, think how to pronounce it. Use the *Guide to Pronunciation*, if necessary.

aisle   \ _____ \

Dictionary of Basic English

The Phonetic Spelling

A. Directions: Phonetic spellings are given as an aid to pronunciation. They are found in slashes after each entry word in the dictionary.

Turn to page 16 in your dictionary. Find the phonetic spellings for *backbone* and *bad*. Write the phonetic spelling in the slashes beside each word.

1) **backbone**   _____\\

   bad   _____\\

2) In which word is the phonetic spelling the same as the real spelling?

   _____

   Find another word on the same page for which the two spellings are the same.

3) The word is _____.

   The phonetic spelling is _____\\.

4) Are the remaining words on page 16 and their phonetic spellings the same or are they different?

   They are _____

B. Directions: Phonetic spellings are written in phonetic symbols. Phonetic symbols are different from letters in two ways:

- Each phonetic symbol stands for just one sound. Some letters, however, stand for more than one sound.
- Some phonetic symbols have diacritical marks over them, such as a long mark, or one or two dots. Letters do not have diacritical marks.

Write ways phonetic symbols are different from letters.

1) _____

   _____

2) _____

   _____

Dictionary of Basic English

Key Words for Phonetic Symbols

Directions: Turn to the *Guide to Pronunciation* on page ix in your dictionary. Copy the key words for each of these phonetic symbols. Each phonetic symbol stands for just one sound. Circle the letters that are in **boldface type**. The first one has been done for you.

When you are done, look at each phonetic symbol on page ix. Read the words that follow each symbol. Think about the sound of that phonetic symbol.

1) \b\   (b)at, ca(bb)age, jo(b)

2) \d\ _____

3) \h\ _____

4) \l\ _____

5) \m\ _____

6) \n\ _____

7) \p\ _____

8) \r\ _____

9) \t\ _____

10) \v\ _____

11) \w\ _____

12) \y\ _____

    Dictionary of Basic English

Symbols and Sounds

A. Directions: The *Guide to Pronunciation* on page ix has two columns of phonetic symbols. All of them look like letters except the schwa. Some of the phonetic symbols for vowels have a long mark, or one or two dots. Each phonetic symbol stands for just one sound. Some phonetic symbols stand for the sound of digraphs, or two letters that make one sound.

Turn to the *Guide to Pronunciation* in your dictionary. Look at the key words for the phonetic symbol "ch." The **boldface** letters tell you that there are three ways to spell the "ch" sound. Copy the key words for the phonetic symbol "ch." Circle the **boldface** letters.

1) ch _____

Find these words in your dictionary. Write each phonetic spelling.

2) child _____\\

3) catch _____\\

4) picture _____\\

Notice that "ch" is always used in the phonetic spelling even though that sound is spelled *ch, tch,* or *tu* in the entry words. For each sound, there is only one phonetic symbol.

B. Directions: Find these words in your dictionary. Write each phonetic spelling.

1) fetch _____\\

2) church _____\\

Not every word that begins with *ch* makes the "ch" sound. Write each phonetic spelling of the words below.

3) chord _____\\

4) chorus _____\\

Dictionary of Basic English

Write the Phonetic Spelling

Directions: Write the phonetic spellings in the slashes beside each of these words.

1) bone \ _____ \

2) damp \ _____ \

3) hang \ _____ \

4) lie \ _____ \

5) milk \ _____ \

6) next \ _____ \

7) pay \ _____ \

8) reed \ _____ \

9) tail \ _____ \

10) vest \ _____ \

11) web \ _____ \

12) yam \ _____ \

13) bus \ _____ \

14) dive \ _____ \

15) hope \ _____ \

16) loft \ _____ \

17) mess \ _____ \

18) not \ _____ \

19) peat \ _____ \

20) rice \ _____ \

21) tick \ _____ \

22) vote \ _____ \

23) wind \ _____ \

24) yolk \ _____ \

25) Look at the first letter of each word and the first letter in the slashes. Are they the same or different?

_____

Dictionary of Basic English

Symbols for *A*, *E*, *I*, and *O*

A. Directions: The *Guide to Pronunciation* on page ix shows three sounds for the vowel *a*. To help us tell them apart, two of the pronunciation symbols have diacritical marks. The phonetic symbols are:

- \a\ for short *a*
- \ā\ for long *a*
- \ä\ for the *a* usually found before *r* and for the short *o* sound

Use your dictionary to write the phonetic spellings for each of these words.

1) add   _____\

2) art   _____\

3) age   _____\

4) odd   _____\

B. Directions: The *Guide to Pronunciation* shows two "e" sounds: short *e* \e\ and long *e* \ē\. Write the phonetic spelling for each of these words.

1) best   _____\

2) beat   _____\

C. Directions: There are two "i" sounds also: short *i* \i\ and long *i* \ī\. Write the phonetic spelling for each of these words.

1) fish   _____\

2) find   _____\

D. Directions: The *Guide to Pronunciation* shows different "o" sounds. The short "o" symbol is the two-dot "a" \ä\ as discussed. The "o" phonetic symbols are long \ō\ and one-dot \ȯ\. Write the phonetic spelling for each of these words.

1) old   _____\

2) off   _____\

Dictionary of Basic English

Symbols for *U* and *E*

A. Directions: The *Guide to Pronunciation* on page ix in your dictionary shows four "u" sounds. The phonetic symbols are: \ü\, \u̇\, \yü\, and \yu̇\. Copy the key words for each symbol.

1) \ü\ _____

2) \u̇\ _____

3) \yü\ _____

4) \yu̇\ _____

For words having the \ü\ and \u̇\ sounds, look in your dictionary for words beginning with *to-*. Check the phonetic spellings for the correct "u" sounds. For the \yü\ and \yu̇\ sounds, look in the *u* section of your dictionary.

The one remaining vowel phonetic symbol is the schwa \ə\. Write the key words for the schwa on the lines below.

5) _____

B. Directions: Write the phonetic spelling of each word.

1) about _____\

2) germ _____\

3) circus _____\

4) mother _____\

5) puppet _____\

Say the key words for each of the phonetic symbols on this page. Think of the sound that the phonetic symbol represents.

Dictionary of Basic English

Matching Vowel Sounds

Directions: Look up each word in your dictionary and write its phonetic spelling. In Column A write the correct letter of the word in Column B that has the same vowel sound. The matching words will have the same phonetic symbol for the vowel. Then, read each pair of words. Think about the vowel sound you hear and the phonetic symbol for that sound.

Column A

____ 1) pipe _____\\

____ 2) rule _____\\

____ 3) talk _____\\

____ 4) use _____\\

____ 5) gold _____\\

____ 6) cent _____\\

____ 7) art _____\\

____ 8) reach _____\\

____ 9) lag _____\\

____10) fame _____\\

____11) good _____\\

____12) pure _____\\

Column B

A) edge _____\\

B) plan _____\\

C) knot _____\\

D) bull _____\\

E) cure _____\\

F) lace _____\\

G) fume _____\\

H) tooth _____\\

I) quote _____\\

J) kite _____\\

K) bee _____\\

L) straw _____\\

Dictionary of Basic English

Symbols for Hard and Soft G

A. Directions: The letter *g* has two sounds, hard "g" as in *get* and soft "g" as in *germ*. The letter *j* has one sound. It is the same as soft "g." Turn to the *Guide to Pronunciation* on page ix in your dictionary. Copy the key words for the phonetic symbols \g\ and \j\.

1) \g\ _____

2) \j\ _____

B. Directions: Find the following words in your dictionary. Write each phonetic spelling.

1) game _____\

2) goat _____\

3) gulf _____\

4) gem _____\

5) gin _____\

6) gym _____\

7) jail _____\

8) jet _____\

9) jaw _____\

C. Directions: Write two more words in which *g* sounds like *j*.

1) _____

2) _____

3) The letter *g* often makes the _____ sound when it comes before the vowels *a, o,* or *u*.

4) The letter *g* often makes the _____ sound when it comes before the vowels *e, i,* or *y*.

Dictionary of Basic English

Symbols for Hard and Soft C

A. Directions: The letter *c* has no sound of its own. That is why *c* is not shown as a phonetic symbol in the *Guide to Pronunciation* on page ix in your dictionary.

This exercise will help you find out which phonetic symbols are used for words that begin with *c*. Write the key words for the phonetic symbols. Underline the letters that are in **boldface type.**

1) \k\ _____   2) \s\   _____

B. Directions: Find the following words in your dictionary. Write each phonetic spelling between the slashes.

1) keep \ _____ \   4) cast   \ _____ \

2) kid   \ _____ \   5) coal   \ _____ \

3) kite \ _____ \   6) cup   \ _____ \

7) In the above phonetic spellings, what phonetic symbol stands for either a *k* or a *c*?

_____

8) What vowels follow the *c* in the above words? _____

C. Directions: Find the following words in your dictionary. Write each phonetic spelling between the slashes.

1) salt \ _____ \   4) cease   \ _____ \

2) sore \ _____ \   5) civil   \ _____ \

3) suit \ _____ \   6) cylinder \ _____ \

7) In the above phonetic spellings, what phonetic symbol stands for either an *s* or a *c*?

_____

8) What vowels follow the *c* in the above words? _____

9) When *c* is followed by *a, o,* or *u,* the phonetic symbol is usually _____\

10) When *c* is followed by *e, i,* or *y,* the phonetic symbol is usually _____\

Dictionary of Basic English

Consonant Digraphs

A. Directions: Turn to the *Guide to Pronunciation* on page ix in your dictionary. Then copy the key words for the following phonetic symbols.

1) \hw\ _____   **3)** \th\ _____

2) \sh\ _____   **4)** \th\ _____

B. Directions: Look up these words in your dictionary. Copy the phonetic spelling of each word.

1) whip   _____\   **5)** awhile   _____\

2) she   _____\   **6)** nation   _____\

3) thing _____\   **7)** bath   _____\

4) that   _____\   **8)** rather   _____\

9) Each of the phonetic symbols above stands for just one sound. Study the underlined letters. Which one of the sounds can be spelled more than one way?

_____

C. Directions: Say the words *thing* and *that*. Are the sounds of *th* alike or different?

1) They are _____

Say the words again slowly.

2) In which word is the "th" sound whispered? _____

3) In which word is the "th" sound voiced? _____

4) Write one word in which the *th* sounds the same as in *thing* and *bath*.

_____

5) Write one word in which the *th* sounds the same as in *that* and *rather*.

_____

Dictionary of Basic English

Syllables With Accent Marks

Directions: The phonetic spelling is separated into syllables according to the way it is pronounced. This is sometimes different from the syllable division of the entry word. Accent marks show which syllables are spoken with more stress. Some syllables are in **boldface type** with a heavy accent, some have a light accent, and some have no accent. But, every word of two or more syllables has at least one accented syllable.

Use the information above to answer these questions.

1) How is a phonetic spelling divided into syllables?_____

_____

2) Is syllable division of the phonetic spelling the same as in the entry word? _____

_____

3) What do the accent marks show? _____

_____

4) Which words have at least one accented syllable?_____

_____

5) Look up the word *aspect* in your dictionary. Notice that one syllable has a heavy accent and the other has a light accent. Put the accent marks on the phonetic spelling below. Underline the heavily accented syllable.

as • pect /as pekt/

Is the heavier accent on the first or the second syllable? _____

Dictionary of Basic English

Accented Syllables

Directions: Read the section on *Pronunciation* on page vi in your dictionary. Then, look up these words in the dictionary and put the heavy or light accent in the phonetic spellings where they belong. Underline the heavily accented syllable.

Words	Phonetic Spellings
1) dark • ness	\ därk nəs \
2) pre • vail	\ pri vāl \
3) tai • lor	\ tā lər \
4) broad • cast	\ bròd kast \
5) short • age	\ shòrt ij \
6) sa • lute	\ sə lüt \
7) lon • gi • tude	\ län jə tüd \
8) a • quar • i • um	\ ə kwer ē əm \
9) fa • vor • ite	\ fā və rət \
10) dec • o • rate	\ dek ə rāt \
11) pop • u • la • tion	\ päp yə lā shən \
12) ve • loc • i • ty	\ və läs ət ē \

Try to pronounce each of the words above. First, figure out how to pronounce each syllable. Then, stress the syllables that have an accent mark. A **boldface** syllable and heavy accent mark show more stress than a light accent mark. Practice until you can read the list of words correctly.

Dictionary of Basic English

Functions of the Parts of Speech

Directions: Read the section on *Word Meanings* that begins on page vi in your dictionary. Become familiar with the work of each part of speech. It will help you to recognize how words are used in your reading. Then, write the function or use of each part of speech as it is given on the page. The first one has been done for you.

Parts of Speech	Function or Use
1) noun	*Names a person, place, or thing*
2) verb	_____
	_____
3) pronoun	_____
	_____
4) adjective	_____
	_____
5) adverb	_____
	_____
6) preposition	_____
	_____
7) conjunction	_____
	_____
8) interjection	_____
	_____

Dictionary of Basic English

Many Parts of Speech

Directions: Some words are used as only one part of speech. But other words stand for two or more parts of speech. Because words can stand for many parts of speech, you must pay attention when looking for the meaning of a word.

Look up the following words in your dictionary. Check each entry for the parts of speech it can be used as. Write them on the lines provided. The first one has been done for you.

Entry Words   **Parts of Speech**

1) lock   _____*noun and verb*_____

2) since   _____

3) overthrow   _____

4) near   _____

5) minus   _____

6) last   _____

7) quack   _____

8) nearby   _____

9) right   _____

10) there   _____

11) key   _____

Dictionary of Basic English

Choosing the Correct Part of Speech

Directions: The word *quiver* is defined on page 180 in your dictionary. Look at the parts of speech *quiver* is used as. Write the part of speech *quiver* is used as in each of the following sentences. Your answer must be one of the parts of speech listed in the dictionary entry for *quiver*. The first one has been done for you.

Part of Speech

1) When she opened the gift, she <u>quivered</u> with joy.   *verb*

2) Jamal took an arrow from the <u>quiver</u>.   _____

3) The wind made the leaves <u>quiver</u>.   _____

4) Paul wore the <u>quiver</u> of arrows on his back.   _____

5) Put this arrow into the <u>quiver</u>.   _____

6) When Juana is nervous, her hand <u>quivers</u>.   _____

7) The branches <u>quivered</u> as the storm came near.   _____

8) The <u>quivers</u> were filled with arrows.   _____

Dictionary of Basic English

Words With Endings

Directions: Inflected forms of words are words with endings.

Turn in your dictionary to *Words With Endings* on page vii. Read to the end of the section on *Verbs* on page viii to find which parts of speech have endings and what purpose the endings serve. Then in the first column below, write the parts of speech that can have endings. In the second column, write the common endings that can be added to each part of speech. In the third column, tell what purpose the endings serve, or what they show.

Parts of Speech	Endings	What the Endings Show
1) _____	_____	_____
2) _____	_____	_____
3) _____	_____	_____
4) _____	_____	_____

Regular Inflected Forms

Directions: The rules for adding endings to regular words are given below. Each rule is followed by a short exercise. Fill in each blank with the correct form.

Rule 1: Nouns usually form the plural by adding *-s*. Nouns ending in *-ch, -sh, -s, -ss, -x,* or *-zz* add *-es* to form the plural.

Singular	Plural	Singular	Plural
1) paper	_____	5) tax	_____
2) chair	_____	6) witch	_____
3) dog	_____	7) sash	_____
4) street	_____	8) grass	_____

Rule 2: Adjectives and adverbs usually add *-er* to the positive to form the comparative and *-est* to form the superlative.

Positive	Comparative	Superlative
9) quick	_____	_____
10) bright	_____	_____
11) fast	_____	_____
12) hard	_____	_____

Rule 3: Regular verbs add *-ed* to the present tense to form the past tense and past participle. They add *-ing* to form the present participle.

Present Tense	Past Tense and Past Participle	Present Participle
13) halt	_____	_____
14) test	_____	_____
15) leap	_____	_____
16) crack	_____	_____

Dictionary of Basic English

Irregular Inflected Forms of Words

Directions: Words that do not follow the rules for adding endings are called irregular inflected forms.

Read the section *Adjectives and Adverbs* on page vii in your dictionary. Pay close attention to the spelling rules given. Many words become irregular when endings are added. Think about the rules. Then, try to write the rules so that they will help you to remember how some words are irregular when endings are added.

Rule 1: _____

_____

_____

Rule 2: _____

_____

_____

Rule 3: _____

_____

_____

Dictionary of Basic English

Irregular Adjectives and Adverbs

Directions: Write the comparative and superlative forms of each adjective. Tell which spelling rule was followed in adding the ending. The first one has been done for you.

Positive	Comparative	Superlative	Spelling Rule Followed
1) flat	*flatter*	*flattest*	*Double the final consonant.*
2) sorry			
3) stable			
4) cozy			
5) feeble			
6) red			

There are only a few irregular adverbs. Here is one of them.

7) early			

Dictionary of Basic English

Final Y Spelling Rule

Directions: Read pages vii and viii in your dictionary. Then, complete the exercises.

1) When an adjective ends in -*y* and a consonant comes before it, -*y* is changed to

   _____ before adding _____ or _____ to
   form the comparative and superlative forms.

Write the comparative and superlative forms of these words:

Positive	Comparative	Superlative
2) merry	_____	_____
3) silly	_____	_____
4) noisy	_____	_____
5) funny	_____	_____
6) easy	_____	_____

Complete this sentence.

7) When a noun ends in -*y* and a consonant comes before it, change the -*y* to
   _____ before adding _____ to form the plural.

Write the plural form of these nouns.

Singular	Plural
8) library	_____
9) ferry	_____
10) body	_____
11) guppy	_____
12) canary	_____

Dictionary of Basic English

Irregular Inflected Nouns

Directions: Nouns form the plural in different ways. Regular nouns add *-s* or *-es* to the singular form. Irregular nouns may follow a spelling rule, use a form from a foreign language, or change the base word.

Look up the following nouns in your dictionary. Write the plural form of each noun. Think how each plural was formed.

Singular	Plural
1) variety	_____
2) corps	_____
3) goose	_____
4) quiz	_____
5) man	_____
6) spectrum	_____
7) child	_____
8) staff	_____
9) battery	_____
10) mouse	_____
11) cargo	_____

     Dictionary of Basic English

Regular and Irregular Verbs

Directions: Read page viii at the beginning of your dictionary. Then, complete these exercises.

1) Verbs regularly add _____ to the present tense to form the past tense and

the past participle, and _____ to form the present participle.

2) Write the missing forms of these verbs. The first one has been done for you.

Present Tense	Past Tense	Past Participle	Present Participle
work	*worked*	*worked*	*working*
coach	_____	_____	_____
depend	_____	_____	_____
load	_____	_____	_____

3) When a verb ends in *-y* preceded by a consonant, the *-y* is changed to _____
   before adding _____ , except when the ending begins with *-i*.

4) Write the principal parts of these verbs. The first one has been done for you.

Present Tense	Past Tense	Past Participle	Present Participle
multiply	*multiplied*	*multiplied*	*multiplying*
try	_____	_____	_____
deny	_____	_____	_____
spy	_____	_____	_____

Dictionary of Basic English

Final E Spelling Rule

Directions: Read pages vii and viii at the beginning of your dictionary. Then, complete these exercises.

1) When words end in final silent -e, _____ the -e before adding an ending.

Complete the following comparisons. The first one has been done for you.

Positive	Comparative	Superlative
2) noble	*nobler*	*noblest*
3) pale	_____	_____
4) simple	_____	_____
5) pure	_____	_____
6) gentle	_____	_____

Write the principal parts of these verbs. The first one has been done for you.

Present Tense	Past Tense	Past Participle	Present Participle
7) chase	*chased*	*chased*	*chasing*
8) tire	_____	_____	_____
9) score	_____	_____	_____
10) grate	_____	_____	_____
11) love	_____	_____	_____

Write the plural form of each noun.

Singular	Plural
12) flame	_____
13) nose	_____
14) lake	_____
15) giraffe	_____

Dictionary of Basic English

Irregular Verbs

Directions: Write the principal parts of the following irregular verbs. If you are not sure of them, look them up in your dictionary.

Present Tense	Past Tense	Past Participle
1) begin	_____	_____
2) choose	_____	_____
3) drink	_____	_____
4) fall	_____	_____
5) fly	_____	_____
6) go	_____	_____
7) hold	_____	_____
8) lay	_____	_____
9) lie	_____	_____
10) ride	_____	_____
11) show	_____	_____
12) strike	_____	_____
13) think	_____	_____
14) win	_____	_____
15) wind	_____	_____

Dictionary of Basic English

Finding the Part of Speech and Meaning

A. Directions: Carefully read each of the following sentences. Decide the part of speech for *after* in each sentence. Try the meaning for that part of speech in the sentence to see if it makes sense. Then, write the part of speech and the meaning in the correct column. The first one has been done for you.

	Part of Speech	Meaning
1) Come for help <u>after</u> two o'clock.	*preposition*	*later in time*
2) Dora came first and Bill came <u>after</u>.	_____	_____
3) We arrived <u>after</u> the train left.	_____	_____
4) I lost track of my cousin in her <u>after</u> years.	_____	_____

B. Directions: Look up the word *forward* in your dictionary. Find the parts of speech of *forward* and the different meanings it can have in a sentence. Then, decide the part of speech and the meaning of *forward* in each of these sentences.

	Part of Speech	Meaning
1) Ann plays <u>forward</u> on the team.	_____	_____
2) The swift <u>forward</u> motion of the boat excited them.	_____	_____
3) The band marched <u>forward</u> a little faster.	_____	_____
4) Don't be so <u>forward</u> in your remarks.	_____	_____

Dictionary of Basic English

Choosing a Meaning

Directions: Read the dictionary entry for *parade* on page 154. Notice that there are three definitions for *parade* as a noun, and two definitions for *parade* as a verb. After each sentence below, tell whether the word *parade* in that sentence is a noun or a verb. Then, tell the number of the meaning that makes sense in that sentence. The first one has been done for you.

		Noun or Verb?	Number of Meaning
1)	While in Seattle, we saw a wonderful <u>parade</u> in Chinatown.	*noun*	*1*
2)	The horses <u>parade</u> on the Fourth of July.		
3)	The circus <u>parade</u> is coming down Main Street.		
4)	Many people like to <u>parade</u> around in new clothes.		
5)	The general watched the <u>parade</u> of the troops.		
6)	The elephants in the <u>parade</u> made loud trumpet noises.		
7)	The sergeant barked orders to the soldiers on <u>parade</u>.		
8)	Kevan is a drum major in the <u>parade</u>.		
9)	My mother <u>parades</u> as a veteran on Memorial Day.		
10)	Bill sells peanuts during the <u>parade</u>.		

Homographs: Alike but Different

A. Directions: Homographs are dictionary entries that are spelled alike but are different in meaning, and sometimes in pronunciation as well.

Look up these homographs in your dictionary. Copy the phonetic spelling and parts of speech of each word.

	Phonetic Spelling	Part of Speech
1) subject	\ _____ \	_____
2) subject	\ _____ \	_____

Read the meanings of the above words. Then answer these questions.

3) How are the words alike? _____

_____

4) How are the words different? _____

_____

B. Directions: Look up these homographs in your dictionary. Copy the phonetic spelling and parts of speech of each word.

	Phonetic Spelling	Part of Speech
1) light	\ _____ \	_____
2) light	\ _____ \	_____

Read the meanings of the above words. Then answer these questions.

3) How are the words alike? _____

_____

4) How are the words different? _____

_____

Dictionary of Basic English

The Use of Illustrations

Directions: Your dictionary includes many illustrations of words, particularly nouns. An illustration helps you get a clearer meaning of the word. Look up each of these words in your dictionary. Study the illustration. Tell how the illustration helps you. The first one has been done for you.

How the Illustrations Help

1) pulley   *The illustration shows what a pulley looks like when it is in use.*

_____

2) helicopter _____

_____

3) lizard _____

_____

4) serpent _____

_____

Examples Help

A. Directions: In the dictionary entry, examples of how words are used in phrases and sentences help in understanding their meanings.

Find the word *sound* in your dictionary. Notice that it has nine meanings. They include three meanings as an adjective, one as a noun, and five as a verb. Seven of the meanings have examples in brackets. Choose four of the examples given. Write one sentence for each example you chose, using the example as part of the sentence. Circle the example. The first one has been done for you.

1) _Bill put up (a sound house frame) and then boarded it in._ _____

2) _____

3) _____

4) _____

5) _____

B. Directions: Find the word *force* in your dictionary. Notice that it has eight meanings. They include five meanings as a noun, and three as a verb. All eight of the meanings have examples in parentheses. Choose four of the examples given. Write one sentence for each example you chose, using the example as part of the sentence. Circle the example. The first one has been done for you.

1) _If the demonstrators become violent, the police will (force them into the bus.)_

2) _____

3) _____

4) _____

5) _____

Dictionary of Basic English

Adding to the Meaning of Words

Directions: Find the following words in your dictionary. Read the definitions. Choose one
meaning with which you are *least familiar.* Write it on the line beside the word.
Think how you might use each of the words in a sentence with the meaning
you have written.

1) underground _____

_____

2) leg _____

_____

3) wing _____

_____

4) gross _____

_____

5) mess _____

_____

6) yoke _____

_____

Dictionary of Basic English

The Least Familiar Meaning

A. Directions: Find the following words in your dictionary and read the definitions. Choose one meaning for each word with which you are *least familiar*. Write the meaning on the line beside the word.

Words	Least Familiar Meanings
1) adventure	_____
2) groom	_____
3) register	_____
4) deposit	_____
5) check	_____
6) score	_____

B. Directions: Choose three of the above words. Use each word in a sentence. Use the meaning that you wrote as the least familiar meaning.

1) _____

_____

_____

2) _____

_____

_____

3) _____

_____

_____

Dictionary of Basic English

The Most Familiar Meaning

Directions: Look up each of the following words in your dictionary. Use the phonetic spelling to help you pronounce it correctly. Then, read the definitions. Choose a meaning for each word with which you are *most familiar*. Write a sentence using each meaning you choose. The first one has been done for you.

Words	Sentences
1) extend	*Whenever they meet each other, they extend their hands in friendship.*
2) fascinate	
3) fierce	
4) fortune	
5) foul	
6) fowl	
7) freight	
8) fresh	

Dictionary of Basic English

Reading Cardinal Numbers

Directions: Turn to *Cardinal Numbers* in Appendix A, Numbers, on page 281 in your dictionary. Write these numbers in words or numerals, as directed. The first one has been done for you.

1) 26 _____*twenty-six*_____

2) 937 _____

3) 1,586 _____

4) $208,043 _____

5) ninety-four _____

6) seven and three-tenths _____

7) three hundred eighty-seven dollars and twenty cents _____

8) one million, five hundred two thousand, two hundred seventeen _____

Dictionary of Basic English

Reading Ordinal Numbers

Directions: You may find help with this exercise in *Ordinal Numbers,* Appendix A, Numbers, beginning on page 282 in your dictionary. Write these ordinal numbers in words or numerals, as directed. The first one has been done for you.

1) 39th   *thirty-ninth* _____

2) 127th   _____

3) 2,742d   _____

4) 1,000,000th   _____

5) Three thousand, one hundred ninetieth _____

6) Seven hundred eighty-fourth _____

7) Thirty-five thousandth _____

8) One million, six hundred thousandth _____

    Dictionary of Basic English

Personal Pronouns

A. Directions: Turn to Appendix B, Pronouns, on pages 283 and 284 in your dictionary. You will find pronouns listed according to the type of pronouns they are. Complete each sentence with one of these first-person singular personal pronouns: *I, my, mine, me,* and *myself.*

1) I want to frost the cake _____ .

2) Tell _____ about your trip to Europe.

3) The pleasure of your visit is all _____ .

B. Directions: Complete each sentence with one of these third-person plural personal pronouns: *they, their, theirs, them,* and *themselves.*

1) Working together saved _____ time.

2) Half of the profit is _____ .

3) The choir members _____ suggested this song.

C. Directions: Complete each sentence with the correct first-person plural personal pronoun. Choose your answer from the word bank.

Word Bank
we
our
ours
us
ourselves

1) We delivered the orders _____ .

2) Please tell _____ the answer to this puzzle.

3) _____ relatives will arrive at three o'clock.

4) He believed us when _____ told him what happened.

5) _____ playing in the band is important to_____ parents.

D. Directions: Complete each sentence with the correct second-person singular personal pronoun. Choose your answer from the word bank.

Word Bank
you
your
yours
yourself

1) I wish you would return the books _____ .

2) Ann will share the rice cakes with _____ .

3) _____ time in the computer lab is from 1:00 to 2:00 P.M.

4) These pencils are mine and those are_____ .

5) Keep some of these apples for_____ .

Dictionary of Basic English

Demonstrative and Interrogative Pronouns

A. Directions: Fill in each blank with one of these demonstrative pronouns: *this, that, these,* and *those.*

1) _____ is my last tennis lesson.

2) Do you see the last brick building? _____ is where I go to class.

3) _____ are the friends I have been waiting for.

4) _____ is my pen. Is _____ yours?

5) _____ is a wetter spring than usual.

6) There are too many packages for me to manage. I can carry _____ if you

can carry _____.

B. Directions: Fill in each blank with an interrogative pronoun.
Choose your answer from the word bank.

Word Bank
who
which
what
whose
whom

1) _____ is the date today?

2) _____ book bag are you carrying?

3) For _____ did you bake that beautiful cake?

4) _____ needs a ride to the skating rink?

5) I have two cameras, and I never know _____ to use.

6) To _____ did you loan my book?

Dictionary of Basic English

Relative Pronouns

A. Directions: Study the *Relative Pronouns* and *Compound Relative Pronouns* in Appendix A, on page 284 in your dictionary. Complete each sentence with one of the relative pronouns listed. The first one has been done for you.

1) This is the girl _____*whom*_____ I invited to go bowling with us.

2) Send me the people _____ names are on this list.

3) I saw a man yesterday_____ reminds me of Uncle John.

4) These brushes are not _____ the painter wants.

B. Directions: Complete each sentence with one of the compound relative pronouns listed on page 284 in your dictionary.

1) The prize will go to the runner, _____ finishes first.

2) George always orders the largest dish of ice cream, _____ the price.

3) You may choose _____ one you want.

4) Take these men's jackets, _____ they are.

5) Which one of the compound relative pronouns above is used as an adjective?

_____ .

Dictionary of Basic English

The Verb *to Have*

Directions: Turn to page 285 in your dictionary. Read through the six tenses of the verb *to have*. In the column on the left below, write the statement form of the present tense of the verb. In the column on the right, write the question form of the same verb and tense. The first one has been done for you.

Statement Form   **Question Form**

1) _____ *I have.* _____   _____ *Have I?* _____

2) _____   _____

3) _____   _____

4) _____ }   { _____

5) _____   _____

6) _____   _____

7) _____   _____

8) _____   _____

Six Tenses of *to Have*

Directions: Write the tense of the verb used in each of these sentences. The complete verb is underlined for you. You will find the six tenses of the verb *to have* on page 285 in your dictionary. The first one has been done for you.

Sentences	Tense of Verbs
1) By Monday, we <u>shall have had</u> plenty of time to rest.	*future perfect*
2) You <u>will have</u> an answer by ten o'clock.	_____
3) We <u>have</u> two tickets to the game.	_____
4) You <u>had</u> a chance to go swimming yesterday.	_____
5) We <u>have had</u> six days of rain this week.	_____
6) They <u>will have</u> enough food for everyone.	_____
7) She <u>had had</u> piano lessons for many years before she studied voice.	_____

The Verb *to Be*

Directions: Turn to page 285 in your dictionary. Read through the six tenses of the verb *to be*. In the column on the left, write the statement form of the present tense of the verb. In the column on the right, write the question form of the same verb and tense. The first one has been done for you.

Statement Form   **Question Form**

1) _____*I am.*_____   _____*Am I?*_____

2) _____   _____

3) _____ ⎫ _____   _____ ⎧ _____

4) _____ ⎬ _____   _____ ⎨ _____

5) _____ ⎭ _____   _____ ⎩ _____

6) _____   _____

7) _____   _____

8) _____   _____

    Dictionary of Basic English

Six Tenses of *to Be*

Directions: Write the tense of the verb used in each of these sentences. The complete verb is underlined for you. You will find the six tenses of the verb *to be* on page 285 in your dictionary.

Sentences	**Tense of Verbs**

1) We <u>have been</u> here for one hour.　　　　　　　_____

2) I <u>am</u> sure that the bus has left the station.　　_____

3) They <u>will be</u> home in time for lunch.　　　　_____

4) Jessie said that you <u>had been</u> in Florida
before Thanksgiving.　　　　　　　　　　　_____

5) When we leave, she <u>will have been</u> down
that trail more than anyone else.　　　　　　_____

6) Michal and I <u>were</u> at the fairgrounds when it started to rain. _____

Irregular Verbs

A. Directions: Turn to page 286 in your dictionary. This listing of irregular verbs offers a convenient way to study the principal parts of verbs that do not follow the rule for forming the past tense and past participle. Write the principal parts of the following verbs.

Present Tense	Past Tense	Past Participle
1) bring	_____	_____
2) choose	_____	_____
3) ring	_____	_____
4) speak	_____	_____

B. Directions: Follow these directions. Use the back of this sheet if you need to.

1) Write one sentence using the past tense of *break*.   _____

2) Write one sentence using the past participle of *break*.   _____

C. Directions: Turn to page 286 in your dictionary. Find the principal parts of these verbs. Write each principal part in the correct column. Look up any word you do not know.

	Past Tense	Past Participle
1) draw	_____	_____
2) know	_____	_____
3) see	_____	_____

Complete each sentence with one of the verbs used above.

4) Yesterday David _____ a clever cartoon.

5) We have _____ the Johnson family for many years.

6) Do you _____ your lesson for today?

7) Have you _____ the play at the community center?

Dictionary of Basic English

Using Irregular Verbs

Directions: On page 286 in your dictionary, you will find the past tense and past participle for these verbs. Write a sentence for the principal part named for the following verbs.

1) Past tense of *give:* _____

_____

2) Past participle of *give:* _____

_____

3) Past tense of *know:* _____

_____

4) Past participle of *know:* _____

_____

5) Past tense of *rise.* _____

_____

6) Past participle of *rise:* _____

_____

7) Past tense of *speak:* _____

_____

8) Past participle of *speak:* _____

_____

9) Past tense of *spring:* _____

_____

10) Past participle of *spring:* _____

_____

Dictionary of Basic English

Learning to Correct Mispelled Words

A. *Directions:* Look at the pairs of words below. Circle the correct spelling. Then look at Appendix D on page 287 in your dictionary to correct the words you did not know.

1) skillful, skillfull

2) lightning, lightening

3) nickle, nickel

4) privlidge, privilege

5) government, goverment

6) disapear, disappear

7) doctor, docter

8) acquaint, aquaint

9) occurred, ocurred

10) film, filme

11) grammar, grammer

12) usuaully, usually

13) resistance, resistence

14) judgement, judgment

15) beatiful, beautiful

B. *Directions:* Look at Appendix D again. Choose ten words that are different from those in Part A. Use each word you choose in a sentence. Use the back of this sheet or a separate sheet of paper.

1) _____

2) _____

3) _____

4) _____

5) _____

6) _____

7) _____

8) _____

9) _____

10) _____

Dictionary of Basic English

Words That Cause Trouble

Directions: Use Appendix D on page 287 in your dictionary to find the ten misspelled words in the paragraph. Circle the misspelled words. Then write the correct spellings on the lines below.

My uncle Ramón is quite a carecter. Onse, when he was fourty, his children wanted to give him a party. (His birthday is in Febuary.) My uncle thought it would be intresting to dress in wierd clothes. Finely, he showed up at the table. He had dressed like a clown. He thought his family would think it was funny. Then he noticed people there who were not his family. He saw his boss and secritary from work and all his neighbors. It was a surprise party. Everyone stared at him. Did it embbarass him? Only for a minite. Then he laughed, sat down, and ate some cake. Everyone had a good time.

1) _____   6) _____

2) _____   7) _____

3) _____   8) _____

4) _____   9) _____

5) _____   10) _____

Unit 1 Mastery Test

A. Directions: Fill in each blank with the letter that comes *between* the two given letters.

1) h ____ j

2) c ____ e

3) p ____ r

4) b ____ d

5) f ____ h

6) t ____ v

7) o ____ q

8) j ____ l

9) s ____ u

B. Directions: Fill in the letters that come *before* and *after* each given letter

1) ____ r ____

2) ____ c ____

3) ____ t ____

4) ____ k ____

5) ____ s ____

6) ____ f ____

7) ____ x ____

8) ____ l ____

9) ____ w ____

10) ____ m ____

11) ____ d ____

12) ____ p ____

C. Directions: Fill in each blank to complete this alphabet.

a ____ ____ d ____ ____ ____ h ____ ____ ____ l ____

____ ____ ____ q ____ ____ t ____ ____ w ____ ____ z

D. Directions: Write the alphabet on the lines below.

_____

_____

_____

_____

_____

Dictionary of Basic English

Unit 2 Mastery Test

A. Directions: Fill in the letters that come *before* and *after* each given letter.

1) ___ p ___   4) ___ x ___

2) ___ f ___   5) ___ r ___

3) ___ h ___   6) ___ d ___

B. Directions: Write these words in alphabetical order.

flour   1) _____

flame   2) _____

ply   3) _____

chin   4) _____

feet   5) _____

giant   6) _____

floor   7) _____

flake   8) _____

C. Directions: On the line before each word, write *Yes* if the word falls alphabetically between the guide words. Write *No* if the word does not fall between the guide words.

Guide words: *compete* and *confine*

1) _____ compute   7) _____ concrete

2) _____ conflict   8) _____ compass

3) _____ consist   9) _____ concert

4) _____ compare   10) _____ comrade

5) _____ complex   11) _____ condense

6) _____ commit

Dictionary of Basic English

Unit 3 Mastery Test

A. *Directions:* Count the number of syllables in each word. Write the number on the line in front of the word.

1) _____ do • mes • tic

2) _____ ge • og • ra • phy

3) _____ clas • si • fi • ca • tion

4) _____ e • mer • gen • cy

5) _____ re • source

6) _____ gov • ern • ment

7) _____ thought • ful

8) _____ in • ev • i • ta • ble

9) _____ zo • di • ac

B. *Directions:* Write *Yes* on the line beside each word if it may be hyphenated at the raised dot at the end of a line of writing. Write *No* if the word may not be hyphenated at the raised dot. If your answer is *No*, tell why not.

	Yes or No?	If No, Why Not?
1) chest • nut	_____	_____
2) hand • y	_____	_____
3) calm • er	_____	_____
4) tick • et	_____	_____
5) u • nit	_____	_____
6) com • ic	_____	_____

Dictionary of Basic English

Unit 4 Mastery Test

A. Directions: Letters are underlined in the words below. In each set, match the words in Column A and Column B whose underlined letters have the same sound. Write the letter of the word on the line before each number. The first one has been done for you.

Set 1		Set 2		Set 3	
Column A	Column B	Column A	Column B	Column A	Column B
_D_ 1) oat	A) in	___ 1) ditch	A) circle	___ 1) pure	A) poor
___ 2) aid	B) coin	___ 2) cake	B) jelly	___ 2) fuse	B) boil
___ 3) it	C) paw	___ 3) photo	C) kite	___ 3) joy	C) moon
___ 4) plow	D) old	___ 4) ginger	D) chin	___ 4) new	D) town
___ 5) cloth	E) aim	___ 5) seal	E) nowhere	___ 5) mouse	E) fume
___ 6) boil	F) bough	___ 6) while	F) staff	___ 6) tour	F) bureau

B. Directions: On the line beside each word, write *First* if the word should be spoken with stress on the first syllable. Write *Second* if the word should be spoken with stress on the second syllable.

1) com • mit \kə mit'\ _____

2) res • cue \res' kyü\ _____

3) en • tire \in tīr'\ _____

4) grate • ful \grāt' fəl\ _____

5) a • sleep \ə slēp'\ _____

6) ar • tist \ärt' əst\ _____

7) lan • tern \lant' ərn\ _____

C. Directions: Look at the following phonetic pronunciations. Correctly write the word on the line following the pronunciation.

1) \chām' bər\ _____

2) \zü\ _____

3) \ak' shən\ _____

D. Directions: Read and follow the directions below.

1) The symbol \ə\ is called _____ .

2) Circle the word with the sound of the phonetic symbol \th\: rather, bath

Dictionary of Basic English

Unit 5 Mastery Test

A. Directions: Write the part of speech for each function listed below.

Part of Speech

1) Describes a verb, adjective, or other adverb   _____

2) Joins words, phrases, or clauses.   _____

3) Names a person, place, or thing.   _____

4) Takes the place of a noun.   _____

5) Shows action or state of being.   _____

6) Shows the relationship between the noun or
   pronoun that follows it and some other word
   in the sentence.   _____

7) An exclamation showing an emotion like surprise.   _____

8) Describes a noun or pronoun.   _____

B. Directions: Write the part of speech for the underlined word in each of these sentences.

Part of Speech

1) They ate the whole <u>bunch</u> of grapes.   _____

2) Please help me to <u>bunch</u> these twigs.   _____

3) Paul bought a used <u>saddle</u> at the shop.   _____

4) I have been <u>saddled</u> with buying the groceries.   _____

5) My uncle has a good <u>command</u> of French.   _____

6) I <u>command</u> you to read to me!   _____

7) They <u>panned</u> for gold with no success.   _____

Dictionary of Basic English

Unit 6 Mastery Test

A. Directions: Complete these sentences.

    1) An inflected form of a word is a word with _____.

    2) Two endings that may be added to a word to form a plural
       are _____and _____.

    3) The plural form of *test* is _____.

    4) The plural form of *library* is _____.

    5) The plural form of *corps* is _____.

    6) The past tense of *walk* is _____.

    7) The past tense of *glide* is _____.

    8) The past tense of *wrap* is _____.

B. Directions: Write the three spelling rules that tell why some inflected forms of words
          are irregular.

    1) _____

    2) _____

    3) _____

C. Directions: Write the comparative and superlative forms of these adjectives.

		Comparative	Superlative
1)	pure	_____	_____
2)	greedy	_____	_____
3)	sad	_____	_____
4	snug	_____	_____

D. Directions: Circle the correct form of the past tense of each of these verbs.

Present Tense	**Past Tense**
1) ride	rode, rided
2) fall	fell, falled
3) load	lid, loaded
4) multiply	multiplyed, multiplied
5) depend	depand, depended

Dictionary of Basic English

Unit 7 Mastery Test

A. Directions: Read the meanings of the words below. For each sentence, write the number of the meaning that makes sense in that sentence.

> **ab • sorb** \əb sōrb'\ *verb* **1.** to take in or soak up
> <*absorb* the water> **2.** to take over <*absorb* our interest>

**Number of
the Meaning**

1) The dry soil <u>absorbed</u> water like a sponge. _____

2) Cotton shirts <u>absorb</u> perspiration. _____

3) She was so <u>absorbed</u> in her book that she didn't hear the telephone ring. _____

4) We tried to <u>absorb</u> the children in a game. _____

> **prop • er • ty** \prä' pərt ē\ *noun, plural* **prop • er • ties**
> **1.** a characteristic or trait <coldness is a *property* of ice.>
> **2.** something that is owned <The house is her *property*.>

5) They were studying the <u>properties</u> of silver. _____

6) One <u>property</u> of a triangle is that it has three sides. _____

7) The Grant family bought <u>property</u> on the island. _____

8) I bought <u>property</u> in town as an investment. _____

9) Attraction to iron is a <u>property</u> of a magnet. _____

> **whole** \hōl\ *adjective* **1.** sound, unchanged, and undam-
> aged <box of *whole* cloves> **2.** having all its members or
> parts <the *whole* collection>\

10) We ate the <u>whole</u> set of ribs. _____

11) Sam bought a <u>whole</u> apple. _____

12) The <u>whole</u> world is big. _____

B. Directions: Answer these questions.

1) What are homographs? _____

2) How do illustrations help a reader to get a clearer idea of the meaning of a word?

_____

3) Why are examples used in a dictionary entry? _____

_____

Dictionary of Basic English

Unit 8 Mastery Test

A. *Directions:* Follow the directions below.

1) List two new words you have learned in the last two weeks._____
   _____

2) Write two sentences using the two words._____
   _____

3) Are you listing new words you find? If yes, how many have you found? _____

4) Describe one way that you are adding new words to your vocabulary. _____
   _____

5) Reading literature every day helps to improve vocabulary. You encounter certain
   words over and over. What literature have you read recently for enjoyment?
   _____
   _____

B. *Directions:* On the lines below, write one complete sentence for each meaning given.
   Use each word as the correct part of speech.

1) **com • pose** \kəm pōz'\ *verb* **com • posed; com • pos • ing** to be made up of
   _____

2) **gnaw** \nȯ\ *verb* to eat away a little at a time _____
   _____

3) **slice** \slīs\ *noun* a thin, broad piece of something _____
   _____

4) **rust • y** \rəs' tē\ *adjective* **rust • i • er; rust • i • est** out of practice _____
   _____

5) **wea • ry** \wīr' ē\ *adjective* **wea • ri • er; wea • ri • est** tired, worn out_____
   _____

Dictionary of Basic English

Unit 9 Mastery Test

A. Directions: Follow the directions below.

1) Write this number in words: 5,792 _____

2) Write in numerals: ten thousand, four hundred thirty-seven and two-tenths_____

3) Write this number in words: 846th _____

B. Directions: In each blank, use *she, her, herself* or *he, him, his, himself.*

1) It was _____ first vacation.

2) She drove _____ family's car.

3) Joseph wanted to wrap the gifts _____ .

4) _____ knew that it was _____ turn to bat the ball.

5) He planned the trip _____ .

C. Directions: Use *who, whose,* or *whom* in these sentences:

1) _____ telephoned you last evening?

2) Point out the person _____ billfold I found.

3) To _____ should I give this box?

4) Tell me _____ is coming.

D. Directions: Write the principal parts of these verbs.

Present Tense	Past Tense	Past Participle
1) catch	_____	_____
2) build	_____	_____
3) walk	_____	_____

E. Directions: Circle the correctly spelled word in each of the following pairs.

1) false, falsse   4) sargent, sergeant

2) benefet, benefit   5) similar, simular

3) atheletic, athletic

Teacher's Guide Answer Key

Activities

Activity 1—The Alphatape

The alphatape may be used if students are having difficulty remembering the alphabet. Direct students to cut out the alphabet on the broken lines and tape the pieces together.

Activity 2—The Alphabet Song

If students are having difficulty remembering the alphabet, pass out copies of the "Alphabet Song." Explain to students that singing the letters should improve memory.

Activity 3—Learning to Alphabetize

A: a b c d e f g h i j k l m n o p q r s t u v w x y z

B: 1) i **2)** h **3)** v **4)** o **5)** e **6)** m **7)** n **8)** d **9)** x **10)** q **11)** u **12)** r **13)** f **14)** c **15)** w **16)** s **17)** b **18)** l **19)** p **20)** k **21)** y **22)** j **23)** g **24)** t

Activity 4—Alphabetical Order: Letters

A: 1) s **2)** n **3)** v **4)** m **5)** w **6)** l **7)** j **8)** b **9)** c **10)** p **11)** e **12)** y **13)** g **14)** t **15)** q **16)** x **17)** r **18)** u **19)** o **20)** f **21)** d **22)** k **23)** h **24)** i

B: a b c d e f g h i j k l m n o p q r s t u v w x y z

C: a b c d e f g h i j k l m n o p q r s t u v w x y z

Activity 5—The Most Familiar Meaning

Note to the teacher: Choice of sentences will vary.

Activity 6—Alphabetical Order: Words

Set 1: brave, civil, guide, letter, parade, route

Set 2: announce, cause, hammer, near, orbit, report

Set 3: bench, purple, tender, unit, vacant, wine

Set 4: camel, fin, laundry, mistake, note, plane

Activity 7—Alphabetizing Words

alley, basic, clay, diary, elbow, fare, idea, low, mail, nickel, rip, serve, trunk, week, zipper

Activity 8—Words With the Same First Letter

Set 1: beetle, birthday, bluff, bowl, bring, button, by

Set 2: dance, dear, dinner, dome, drum

Activity 9—Alphabetical Order by Second Letter

Set 1: cavity, cent, civil, class, cough, curve

Set 2: gauge, gentle, ginger, govern, guide, gym

Set 3: bake, bend, blanket, book, brave, bundle

Set 4: magic, mention, mind, mole, mustard, myth

Activity 10—Alphabetical Order by Third Letter

Set 1: lobster, lodge, lofty, long, loud, love

Set 2: today, toe, together, toll, tomato, topic, torch

Activity 11—Using the Fourth Letter to Alphabetize

Set 1: spoil, spoke, spool, sport, spot, spout

Set 2: theater, their, then, there, these, they

Activity 12—Learning About Guide Words

A: 1) No **2)** Yes **3)** No **4)** Yes **5)** Yes **6)** No **7)** No **8)** No **9)** Yes **10)** Yes

B: 1) No **2)** Yes **3)** No **4)** Yes **5)** Yes **6)** No **7)** No **8)** No **9)** Yes **10)** Yes

Activity 13—Use the Guide Words

Set 1: 1) No **2)** Yes **3)** Yes **4)** No **5)** Yes **6)** Yes **7)** No **8)** No **9)** Yes **10)** No

Set 2: 1) No **2)** Yes **3)** No **4)** No **5)** Yes **6)** No **7)** Yes **8)** Yes **9)** No **10)** Yes

Activity 14—Dividing Words Into Syllables

1) flan • nel, 2 **2)** grass • hop • per, 3 **3)** fic • tion, 2 **4)** choc • o • late, 3 **5)** main • ten • ance, 3 **6)** ra • di • a • tion, 4 **7)** sur • vi • val, 3 **8)** hand • writ • ing, 3 **9)** build • ing, 2 **10)** tri • umph, 2

Activity 15—Counting Syllables

1) a • bil • i • ty, 4 **2)** di • no • saur, 3 **3)** dome, 1 **4)** ker • o • sene, 3 **5)** o • be • di • ence, 4 **6)** pad • dle, 2 **7)** pop • u • la • tion, 4 **8)** por • poise, 2 **9)** ul • tra • vi • o • let, 5 **10)** wind • mill, 2

Activity 16—Syllable Division and Hyphenation

1) Yes **2)** No. Don't separate a one-letter syllable from the rest of the word. **3)** Yes **4)** No. Don't separate a one-letter syllable from the rest of the word. **5)** Yes **6)** No. Don't separate a one-letter syllable from the rest of the word. **7)** Yes **8)** Yes

Activity 17—Using Hyphens

1) Yes **2)** No. Don't separate a two-letter ending from the word. **3)** Yes **4)** No. Don't separate a one-letter syllable from the rest of the word. **5)** No. Don't separate a one-syllable ending from the word. **6)** Yes **7)** Yes **8)** Yes

Activity 18—Phonetic Spellings

A: 1) Phonetic spellings are given as an aid to pronunciation. **2)** They are found in slashes after each entry word in the dictionary. **3)** The phonetic spelling is written in symbols. **4)** The phonetic symbols are listed in the Guide to

Pronunciation and at the bottom of every two-page spread in the dictionary. **5)** In the key words are letters in **bold-face type** that have the sound of the phonetic symbol.

B: \īl\

Activity 19—The Phonetic Spelling

A: 1) \bak' bōn\   \bad\ **2)** bad **3)** bag \bag\
4) different

B: 1) Each symbol stands for just one sound. Some letters, however, stand for more than one sound. **2)** Some phonetic symbols have diacritical marks over them, such as a long mark, or one or two dots. Letters do not have diacritical marks.

Activity 20—Key Words for Phonetic Symbols

1) (b)at, ca(bb)age, jo(b) **2)** (d)og, pa(d) **3)** (h)and, be(h)ave
4) (l)itt(l)e, (l)ive(l)y **5)** (m)other, ho(m)e **6)** (n)ose, li(n)e(n)
7) (p)a(p)er, shi(p) **8)** (r)un, fu(r) **9)** (t)icke(t), ba(tt)er
10) (v)al(v)e, co(v)er **11)** (w)in, be(w)are **12)** (y)ear, (y)es

Activity 21—Symbols and Sounds

A: 1) (ch)ild, ca(tch), pic(tu)re **2)** \chīld\ **3)** \kach\
4) \pik' chər\

B: 5) \fech\ **6)** \chərch\ **7)** \kȯrd\ **8)** \kȯr' əs\

Activity 22—Write the Phonetic Spelling

1) \bōn\ **2)** \damp\ **3)** \hang\ **4)** \lī\ **5)** \milk\
6) \nekst\ **7)** \pā\ **8)** \rēd\ **9)** \tāl\ **10)** \vest\
11) \web\ **12)** \yam\ **13)** bəs\ **14)** \dīv\ **15)** \hōp\
16) \lȯft\ **17)** \mes\ **18)** \nät\ **19)** \pēt\ **20)** \rīs\
21) \tik\ **22)** \vōt\ **23)** \wind\ or \wīnd\ **24)** \yōk\
25) They are the same.

Activity 23—Symbols for *A, E, I,* and *0*

A: 1) \ad\ **2)** \ärt\ **3)** \āj\ **4)** \äd\ **B: 1)** \best\
2) \bēt\ **C: 1)** \fish\ **2)** \fīnd\ **D: 1)** \ōld\ **2)** \ȯf\

Activity 24—Symbols for *U* and *E*

A: 1) school, tune **2)** book, pull, jury **3)** few, view, music
4) unite, pure **5)** about, germ, circus, mother, puppet

B: 1) \ə baút'\ **2)** \jərm\ **3)** \sər' kəs\ **4)** \məth' ər\
5) \pəp' ət\

Activity 25—Matching Vowel Sounds

1) J \pīp\ \kīt\ **2)** H \rül\ \tüth\ **3)** L \tȯk\ \strȯ\
4) G \yüz\ \fyüm\ **5)** I \gōld\ \kwōt\ **6)** A \sent\ \ej\
7) C \ärt\ \nät\ **8)** K \rēch\ \bē\ **9)** B \lag\ \plan\
10) F \fām\ \lās\ **11)** D \gúd\ \búl\ **12)** E \pyúr\
\kyúr\

Activity 26—Symbols for Hard and Soft *G*

A: 1) girl, tag, tiger **2)** jelly, gym, ridge

B: 1) \gām\ **2)** \gōt\ **3)** \gəlf\ **4)** \jem\ **5)** \jin\
6) \jim\ **7)** \jāl\ **8)** \jet\ **9)** \jȯ\

C: 1) Answers will vary. **2)** Answers will vary. **3)** \g\
4) \j\

Activity 27—Symbols for Hard and Soft C

A: 1) kick, chemical **2)** saucer, face, lesson

B: 1) \kēp\ **2)** \kid\ **3)** \kīt\ **4)** \kast\ **5)** \kōl\
6) \kəp\ **7)** k **8)** a, o, u

C: 1) \sȯlt\ **2** \sȯr\ **3)** \süt\ **4)** \sēs\ **5)** \siv' əl\
6) \sil' ən dər\ **7)** s **8)** e, i, y **9)** k **10)** s

Activity 28—Consonant Digraphs

A: 1) whip, awhile **2)** she, cash, nation **3)** thing, bath
4) that, rather

B: 1) \hwip\ **2)** \shē\ **3)** \thing\ **4)** \that\ **5)** \ə
hwīl'\ **6)** \nā' shən\ **7)** \bath\ **8)** \rath' ər\ **9)** sh

C: 1) different **2)** thing **3)** that

D: Answers will vary.

E: Answers will vary.

Activity 29—Syllables With Accent Marks

A: 1) The phonetic spelling is separated into syllables according to the way it is pronounced. **2)** Syllable division of the phonetic spelling is sometimes different from the syllable division of the entry word. **3)** Accent marks show which syllables are spoken with more stress.
4) Every word of two or more syllables has at least one accented syllable.

B: \as' pekt'\, first

Activity 30—Accented Syllables

1) \därk' nəs\ **2)** \pri vāl'\ **3)** \tā' lər\ **4)** \brȯd' kast'\
5) \shȯrt' ij\ **6)** \sə lüt'\ **7)** \län' jə tüd'\ **8)** \ə kwer'
ē əm\ **9)** \fā' və rət\ **10)** \dek' ə rāt'\ **11)** \päp yə lā'
shən\ **12)** \və läs' ə tē\

Activity 31—Functions of the Parts of Speech

1) Names a person, place, thing, or idea. **2)** Shows action or state of being. **3)** Takes the place of a noun.
4) Describes a noun or pronoun. **5)** Describes a verb, adjective, or other adverb. **6)** Shows the relationship between the noun or pronoun that follows it and some other word in the sentence. **7)** Joins words, phrases, or clauses. **8)** An exclamation showing an emotion such as surprise or happiness.

Activity 32—Many Parts of Speech

1) noun and verb **2)** adverb, preposition, conjunction
3) verb, noun **4)** adverb, preposition, adjective, verb
5) preposition, adjective **6)** adjective, verb, adverb
7) verb, noun, adjective **8)** adverb, adjective **9)** adjective, noun, adverb, verb **10)** adverb, pronoun, noun, interjection **11)** noun, adjective

Activity 33—Choosing the Correct Part of Speech

1) verb **2)** noun **3)** verb **4)** noun **5)** noun **6)** verb
7) verb **8)** noun

Activity 34—Words with Endings

1) noun: -s, -es plural form; -'s, -s' possession 2) verb: -ed, -ing tense 3) adjective: -er, -est comparative and superlative degrees 4) adverb: -er, -est comparative and superlative degrees

Activity 35—Regular Inflected Forms

1) papers 2) chairs 3) dogs 4) streets 5) taxes 6) witches 7) sashes 8) grasses 9) quicker, quickest 10) brighter, brightest 11) faster, fastest 12) harder, hardest 13) halted, halting 14) tested, testing 15) leaped, leaping 16) cracked, cracking

Activity 36—Irregular Inflected Forms of Words

Rule 1: When a word ends in a single consonant preceded by a single vowel, double the consonant before adding the ending. *Rule 2:* When a word ends in silent *e*, drop the *e* before adding an ending that begins with a vowel. *Rule 3:* When a word ends in *y*, change the *y* to *i* before adding an ending, except when the ending begins with *i*.

Activity 37—Irregular Adjectives and Adverbs

1) flatter, flattest. *Rule:* Double the final consonant. 2) sorrier, sorriest. *Rule:* Change y to i. 3) stabler, stablest. *Rule:* Drop the silent e. 4) cozier, coziest. *Rule:* Change y to i. 5) feebler, feeblest. *Rule:* Drop the silent e. 6) redder, reddest. *Rule:* Double the final consonant. 7) earlier, earliest. *Rule:* Change y to i.

Activity 38—Final *Y* Spelling Rule

1) i; -er or -est 2) merrier, merriest 3) sillier, silliest 4) noisier, noisiest 5) funnier, funniest 6) easier, easiest 7) i, -es 8) libraries 9) ferries 10) bodies 11) guppies 12) canaries

Activity 39—Irregular Inflected Nouns

1) varieties 2) corps 3) geese 4) quizzes 5) men 6) spectra or spectrums 7) children 8) staffs or staves 9) batteries 10) mice 11) cargoes or cargos

Activity 40—Regular and Irregular Verbs

1) -ed, -ing 2) worked, worked, working; coached, coached, coaching; depended, depended, depending; loaded, loaded, loading 3) -i, -ed 4) multiplied, multiplied, multiplying; tried, tried, trying; denied, denied, denying; spied, spied, spying

Activity 41—Final *E* Spelling Rule

1) drop 2) nobler, noblest 3) paler, palest 4) simpler, simplest 5) purer, purest 6) gentler, gentlest 7) chased, chased, chasing 8) tired, tired, tiring 9) scored, scored, scoring 10) grated, grated, grating 11) loved, loved, loving 12) flames 13) noses 14) lakes 15) giraffes

Activity 42—Irregular Verbs

1) began, begun 2) chose, chosen 3) drank, drunk 4) fell, fallen 5) flew, flown 6) went, gone 7) held, held 8) laid, laid 9) lay, lain or lied, lied 10) rode, ridden 11) showed, shown 12) struck, struck 13) thought, thought 14) won, won 15) wound, wound

Activity 43—Finding the Part of Speech and Meaning

A: 1) preposition, later in time 2) adverb, behind in time or place 3) conjunction, later than 4) adjective, coming later

B: 1) noun, a player on a team 2) adjective, moving toward the front 3) adverb, onward toward the front 4) adjective, bold and rude

Activity 44—Choosing a Meaning

1) noun, 1 2) verb, 1 3) noun, 3 4) verb, 2 5) noun, 2 6) noun, 3 7) noun, 2 8) noun, 1 9) verb, 1 10) noun, 1

Activity 45—Homographs: Alike but Different

A: 1) \səb' jikt\ noun 2) \səb **jekt'**\ verb 3) They are spelled alike. 4) They have different parts of speech, pronunciation, and meaning.

B: 1) \līt\ noun 2) \līt\ verb 3) They are spelled and pronounced alike. 4) They have different parts of speech and meaning.

Activity 46—The Use of Illustrations

Notes to the teacher: Answers will vary. Possible answers are: 1) The illustration shows what a pulley looks like when it is in use. 2) The illustration shows one clear example of a helicopter. 3) The illustration shows details of the body of the lizard, such as its claws and tail. 4) The illustration shows where a serpent might be found.

Activity 47—Examples Help

Note to the teacher: Accept any reasonable sentences that use the examples correctly.

Activity 48—Adding to the Meaning of Words

Note to the teacher: Sentences will vary.

Activity 49—The Least Familiar Meaning

Note to the teacher: The choice of meanings and sentences will vary.

Activity 50—The Most Familiar Meaning

Note to the teacher: The choice of sentences will vary.

Activity 51—Reading Cardinal Numbers

A: 1) twenty-sixth 2) nine hundred thirty-seven 3) one thousand, five hundred eighty-six, or fifteen hundred eighty-six 4) two hundred eight thousand, forty-three dollars

B: 1) 94 2) 7 3/10, or 7.3 3) $387.20 4) 1,502,217

Activity 52—Reading Ordinal Numbers

A: 1) thirty-ninth **2)** one hundred twenty-seventh
3) two thousand, seven hundred forty-second **4)** one millionth

B: 1) 3,190th **2)** 784th **3)** 35,000th **4)** 1,600,000th

Activity 53—Personal Pronouns

A: 1) myself **2)** me **3)** mine

B: 1) them **2)** theirs **3)** themselves

C: 1) ourselves **2)** us **3)** Our **4)** we **5)** Our, our

D: 1) yourself **2)** us **3)** Your **4)** yours **5)** yourself

Activity 54—Demonstrative and Interrogative Pronouns

Notes to the teacher: This and *that* are sometimes interchangeable. *These* and *those* are also sometimes interchangeable.

A: 1) This **2)** That **3)** These, Those **4)** This, that **5)** This
6) these, those

B: 1) What **2)** Whose **3)** whom **4)** Who **5)** which
6) whom

Activity 55—Relative Pronouns

A: 1) whom **2)** whose **3)** who **4)** what

B: 1) whoever **2)** whatever **3)** whichever **4)** whosever
5) whichever

Activity 56—The Verb *To Have*

1) I have. Have I? **2)** You have. Have you? **3)** He has. Has he? **4)** She has. Has she? **5)** It has. Has it? **6)** We have. Have we? **7)** You have. Have you? **8)** They have. Have they?

Activity 57—Six Tenses of *To Have*

1) future perfect **2)** future **3)** present **4)** past **5)** present perfect **6)** future **7)** past perfect

Activity 58—The Verb *To Be*

1) I am. Am I? **2)** You are. Are you? **3)** He is. Is he?

4) She is. Is she? **5)** It is. Is it? **6)** We are. Are we?
7) You are. Are you? **8)** They are. Are they?

Activity 59—Six Tenses of *To Be*

1) present perfect **2)** present **3)** future **4)** past perfect
5) future perfect **6)** past

Activity 60—Irregular Verbs

A: 1) brought, brought **2)** chose, chosen **3)** rang, rung
4) spoke, spoken

B: 1) Sentences will vary. **2)** Sentences will vary.

C: 1) drew, drawn **2)** knew, known **3)** seen, seen
4) drew, saw **5)** known **6)** know **7)** seen

Activity 61—Using Irregular Verbs

Notes to the teacher: For numbers 1-10, sentences will vary.

Activity 62—Learning to Correct Misspelled Words

A: 1) skillful **2)** lightning **3)** nickel **4)** privilege
5) government **6)** disappear **7)** doctor **8)** acquaint
9) occurred **10)** film **11)** grammar **12)** usually
13) resistance **14)** judgment **15)** beautiful

B: *Note to the teacher:* Sentences will vary.

Activity 63—Words That Cause Trouble

Note to the teacher: The corrected paragraph follows. The words that were misspelled are underlined.

My uncle Ramón is quite a <u>character</u>. <u>Once</u>, when he was <u>forty</u>, his children wanted to give him a party. (His birthday is in <u>February</u>.) My uncle thought it would be <u>interesting</u> to dress in <u>weird</u> clothes. <u>Finally</u>, he showed up at the table. He had dressed like a clown. He thought his family would think it was funny. Then he noticed people there who were not his family. He saw his boss and <u>secretary</u> from work and all his neighbors. It was a surprise party. Everyone stared at him. Did it <u>embarrass</u> him? Only for a <u>minute</u>. Then he laughed, sat down, and ate some cake. Everyone had a good time.

Mastery Tests

Unit 1 Mastery Test

Part A: 1) i **2)** d **3)** q **4)** c **5)** g **6)** u **7)** p **8)** k **9)** t

Part B: 1) qrs **2)** bcd **3)** stu **4)** jkl **)** rst **6)** efg **7)** wxy **8)** klm **9)** vwx **10)** lmn **11)** cde **12)** opq

Part C: a b c d e f g h i j k l m n o p q r s t u v w x y z

Part D: a b c d e f g h i j k l m n o p q r s t u v w x y z

Unit 2 Mastery Test

Part A: 1) opq **2)** efg **3)** ghi **4)** wxy **5)** qrs **6)** cde

Part B: chin, feet, flake, flame, floor, flour, giant, ply

Part C: 1) Yes **2)** No **3)** No **4)** No **5)** Yes **6)** No **7)** Yes **8)** No **9)** Yes **10)** Yes **11)** No

Unit 3 Mastery Test

Part A: 1) 3 **2)** 4 **3)** 5 **4)** 4 **5)** 2 **6)** 3 **7)** 2 **8)** 5 **9)** 3

Part B: 1) Yes **2)** No; Don't separate a one-letter ending from the rest of the word **3)** Yes **4)** Yes **5)** No; Don't separate a one-letter syllable from the rest of the word **6)** Yes

Unit 4 Mastery Test

Part A: Set 1—1) D **2)** E **3)** A **4)** F **5)** C **6)** B; **Set 2—1)** D **2)** C **3)** F **4)** B **5)** A **6)** E; **Set 3—1)** F **2)** E **3)** B **4)** C **5)** D **6)** A

Part B: 1) second **2)** first **3)** second **4)** first **5)** second **6)** first **7)** first

Part C: 1) chamber **2)** zoo **3)** action

Part D: 1) schwa **2)** rather

Unit 5 Mastery Test

Part A: 1) adverb **2)** conjunction **3)** noun **4)** pronoun **5)** verb **6)** preposition **7)** interjection **8)** adjective

Part B: 1) noun **2)** verb **3)** noun **4)** verb **5)** noun **6)** verb **7)** noun

Unit 6 Mastery Test

Part A: 1) an ending **2)** s, es **3)** tests **4)** libraries **5)** corps **6)** walked **7)** glided **8)** wrapped

Part B: *Rule 1:* When a word ends in a single consonant preceded by a single vowel, double the consonant before adding the ending. *Rule 2:* When a word ends in silent *e,* drop the *e* before adding an ending that begins with a vowel. *Rule 3:* When a word ends in *y,* preceded by a consonant, change the *y* to *i* before adding an ending, except when the ending begins with *i.*

Part C: 1) purer, purest **2)** greedier, greediest **3)** sadder, saddest **4)** snugger, snuggest

Part D: 1) rode **2)** fell **3)** loaded **4)** multiplied **5)** depended

Unit 7 Mastery Test

Part A: 1) 1 **2)** 1 **3)** 2 **4)** 2 **5)** 1 **6)** 1 **7)** 2 **8)** 2 **9)** 1 **10)** 2 **11)** 1 **12)** 2

Part B: 1) Homographs are words that are spelled alike but have different meanings, parts of speech, and sometimes different pronunciations. **2)** Illustrations show details that may not be described in words. Illustrations show exactly what the entry word is.
3) Examples are used to show how a word with a particular meaning is used in a phrase or sentence

Unit 8 Mastery Test

Note to the teacher: For all questions, answers will vary. Check to be sure students have used reasonable answers.

Unit 9 Mastery Test

Part A: 1) five thousand, seven hundred ninety-two **2)** 10,437.2, or 10,437 2/10 **3)** eight hundred forty-sixth

Part B: 1) her/his **2)** her **3)** himself **4)** He/She, his/her **5)** himself

Part C: 1) who **2)** whose **3)** whom **4)** who

Part D: 1) caught, has caught **2)** built, has built **3)** walked, has walked

Part E: 1) false **2)** benefit **3)** athletic **4)** sergeant **5)** similar